An Analog Life in a Digital World...

"Christian Devotions on the Lighter Side"

Susan Daniels Poulos

An Analog Life in a Digital World

"Christian Devotions on the Lighter Side"

Susan Daniels Poulos

Published by:
CSNbooks, Inc.
1975 Janich Ranch Ct.
El Cajon, CA 92019
www.CSNbooks.com
1-866-484-6184

Dedication

This book is dedicated to my husband, John Poulos, and to the memory of my parents, Myrt and Howard Daniels. With a great deal of gratitude I thank all three of those people for giving me a great life!

For many of the Devotional Readings in this book I owe a thank you to my father, who wrote a book titled, "Youthful Ideas for Devotions," but died before it could be published. I have taken many of his ideas, reworked them, and updated them with my own interpretations for inclusion in this book.

My purposes in writing this book are three fold: (1) to record some of the experiences I've had in my life, (2) to offer the reader some "thoughts to ponder;" to, perhaps, take to heart and influence their life for the better, and (3) to give glory to my Lord and Savior, Jesus Christ, for a wonderful life!

Table of Contents

Introduction

Stepping Into the Presence of God Almighty

One night, when the moon was full and the stars were big and bright, I stepped into the presence of God Almighty! The night was picture-book perfect...really beautiful! The air was cool and crisp and, as camp employees, we'd gathered on a stone outcropping overlooking a small pond. That night, with the moon so bright you could see everything round about and the moon's reflection sparkling off the small pond below us...there was a hush among the employees as they found comfortable spots and sat down on that stone outcropping.

As we sat there in the hush of that night, the Camp Director began to tell us about a man he knew who thought he had an abundant life. That man, a friend of his, had a good job, a nice wife and a small child, a house virtually paid for, two cars in the garage, a boat, and an RV. Still, the friend had no inner peace and contentment. He was always striving for more!

The Camp Director went on to say that God Almighty had created each of us in His own image. And, while mankind was in the Garden of Eden there was communication and compatibility between God and man. Nevertheless, mankind chose to disobey God and go his own willful way, resulting in a separation from God. The result... within the heart of mankind there developed a "void, or empty spot." Something was missing.

Down through the ages, mankind had tried to fill that empty spot with different things. In the case of the Camp Director's friend, he'd tried to fill that spot with the normal things of this world...things that many people strive for and desire.

But, God Almighty wasn't part of that friend's life and so he was not peaceful nor content. He'd even been accused of road rage and losing his temper at the office. His job was in jeopardy and his wife, often the target of frustrations at home, had been thinking about divorce. The boat and RV no longer interested the friend and he'd considered selling them.

The Camp Director's explanation continued. He said that God had provided a way for mankind to come into His presence and to once again communicate, be compatible with Him, and to be peaceful and content. That way was through Jesus Christ, his Son.

It was, the Camp Director explained, as though God was on one outcropping of rock and his friend was on another. In between those two outcroppings of rock Father God had placed his Son, Jesus Christ. If his friend wanted peace and contentment in his life...he must "cross the space between those two outcroppings of rock" by first coming to know God's Son, Jesus Christ.

A first step in doing that was to ask Christ into his life as his personal Lord and Savior. He needed to admit that he'd made mistakes and that he wanted peace and contentment within himself...that he wanted to fill that "empty spot or void" within his heart...and that he wanted to seek a closer communication and compatibility with God.

The Camp Director explained that God sent Jesus, His Son, to earth to die for his friend...for the mistakes and sins his friend (and all of us) had made in life. And, when Jesus came to earth He knew what His mission was, but He came anyway. He wanted to help the Camp Director's friend...and each of us...to have peace and contentment, plus a closer communication and compatibility with God. That's why Jesus allowed Himself to be crucified on the cross.

But, the Camp Director went on to explain that while Jesus died on the cross for the mistakes and sins of mankind...He rose from the dead...He didn't stay in the grave, but rather ascended into heaven. And just as He had been once before, now once again, He's at the right hand of God, the Father Almighty.

Jesus is called "the light of the world" because He restored mankind back into a place of favor and through Him we can have peace, contentment and a closer communication and compatibility with God.

And, then, on that moonlit night all of us got up from that outcropping of rock and began descending toward the pond at the foot of that rock. There each of us was given a lighted candle in the center of a small block of wood and we were told to line up along the bank of that small pond. Holding our lighted candles, the Camp Director led us in a prayer...a prayer that you, dear reader, might want to pray too:

Dear Lord Jesus, I want inner peace, contentment and a closer communication and compatibility with God Almighty. I admit that I've made some mistakes, committed sins and I ask for forgiveness of those things. I believe that you did come to earth to save mankind (and me!) from sins. I believe that that's why you died upon the cross. I ask you, now, Lord Jesus, to come into my heart and life. I want you to become my Savior and Lord.

Praying that prayer, the Camp Director explained, was the first step in filling that empty spot or void within us. And then he told us that our candles...on that beautiful moonlit night, in that awesome spot...were going to represent Jesus Christ as being the "light of the world." And, so we were instructed to place our blocks of wood and lit candles into the pond and gently stir the water to make them float away from the shoreline.

Many employees prayed that prayer for the first time in their lives that night and became followers of and believers in Jesus Christ.

But, how about you, dear reader...have you prayed that prayer? Is Jesus Christ your Savior and Lord?

Regardless of whether you just prayed that prayer for the first time in your life or you prayed a prayer like it many years ago, the author of this little book invites you to draw closer to Jesus Christ by reading the devotions that follow...

Devotional Reading #1

Shifting Shadows

A foursome of shadows stood in the parking lot of a country club while their human counterparts discussed their recent game of golf. With one eye on the cloud in the distant horizon that would bring about their demise, each shadow began to discuss their human counterpart.

"Joe, my human counterpart," remarked the tallest shadow, "likes to spend all his time here at the country club. His wife and family hardly ever see him."

"Well," said the shadow of Mike, the thirty-something good looker, "my fellow is obsessed with women and has been known to date two in one day…one in the afternoon and a different one at night, and if he doesn't have a date with one, he's surfing the Internet…looking at one."

"Not my guy," responded the shadow of Brian, "he's up to his eyebrows playing the stock market. The first thing he does each morning is see where the market closed the day before and figure out if he made or lost money."

Lastly, the shadow of Jeff spoke up, "I'm the shadow of a guy that's hard to figure out. Jeff seems to enjoy helping people and he's always fixing things for them. He's always kind to people and often defends "the under-dog"…the person who's down on his luck, isn't very attractive, or has been "short changed" in life. Frankly, I can't figure him out!"

If one of those four shadows was replaced by *your* shadow, dear reader…what would be said about you? Would the comments be positive or negative? Would your shadow hold its head high and be proud of what it said or would it be troubled and hang its head?

Robert Louis Stevenson wrote a poem that contained this line: "I have a little shadow that goes in and out with me and what can be the reason for him is more than I can see." So, imagine for a moment that the "shadow that goes in and out" with you and follows you represents something that's constantly seeking out the truth about everyone and everything…that it's trying to decide what's right or wrong. God Almighty (when He's part of our life) has placed a "conscience" in each of us to help us make decisions between right and wrong. This "conscience shadow," unlike the foursome shadows in the parking lot who disappear when a cloud passes overhead blocking out the sun, is always with us!

In the foursome of shadows standing in the parking lot, Jeff's shadow represented the guy with the greatest degree of conscience or a sense of right and wrong.

When Jesus Christ was being crucified on the cross, His shadow fell across several people at the foot of the cross…among them two quite different women. One was His mother, Mary, and the other, Mary Magdalene. Mary, His mother, being a virgin and of the correct family lineage, was chosen of God to conceive (through the Holy Spirit) and to give birth to Jesus. But, Mary Magdalene, on the other hand, was quite a different kind of woman. Jesus had delivered her of seven demons that had infected her. Jesus, through His healing power, had delivered her and made her whole.

Jesus' shadow, as He hung on the cross, may have fallen upon several people that day. And, it's very likely that whomever that shadow fell on was, as a result, changed forever…for all eternity. Some, who responded negatively to Christ, were damned to hell forever, while others, who recognized Jesus as the Son of God were offered eternal life. There was power in His shadow to change lives!

In the New Testament, in Acts 5, we can see that even the apostles of Jesus possessed that power to change lives and heal people. In Acts 5:15-16, it says, *"…they even carried out the sick into the streets, and laid them on beds and pallets, that as Peter came by at least **his shadow*** (emphasis added) *might fall on some of them. The people also gathered from the towns around Jerusalem, bringing* *the sick and those afflicted with unclean spirits, and they were all healed."*

Prayer:
Oh, Lord, help me to always be mindful of where I am, what I'm doing, what I'm thinking or what I'm speaking…that my choices would make my shadow (could it speak) and You, Lord Jesus Christ, proud of me! Help me to remember that "my shadow goes in and out with me" and reflects my presence. I pray that my thoughts and actions are Christ-like in nature. Help me to remember the example of Apostle Peter, whose shadow fell on other people and changed their lives for the better. Develop in me a greater sense of right and wrong and to choose whatever is right! Help me to be constructive in all that I do. Help me to look for and to further the good in people. Furthermore, help me to remember that if I make a mistake, if, in fact, I sin, that Jesus Christ, as my Lord and Savior, has died to set me free from my mistakes and sins. He has forgiven me and will help me to do better in the future!

Amen

Devotional Reading #2

Make a Joyful Noise

There's probably not a single person alive who, if they can hear, doesn't like music of one kind or another. What is your favorite kind of music, dear reader? Do you like the classics, or perhaps jazz is more to your taste. Perhaps you prefer the big band sounds or show tunes, or, having grown up listening to rock music or rap, you wouldn't listen to anything else! Maybe you like pop or hip hop, or maybe country western music sets your feet a'dancin' and is your favorite! What do you prefer, dear reader?

Well, I have to tell you…I love music…many kinds of music! I suppose it all started when, as a girl of ten or eleven, my parents hired a music teacher to teach me how to play the piano. She lived in a small town about twenty five miles from our home and the day of my piano lesson she'd drive her model T car into town and to our house. We'd hear her coming as she "putt…putt…putted along." She was a roly-poly lady with dyed reddish brown hair and white roots, who sat on the piano bench with me and tried to teach me what she knew about playing the piano. After about two years of it, however, we all gave up! I'm afraid I had no aptitude for music!

Many years later, I was dating a fellow who played the baritone ukulele. I was terribly impressed and even more so when he accompanied himself as he sang. He had a good voice and so it was no surprise to me when he told me that musical abilities ran in his family. His mother played the harmonica, his sister was a professional banjo player, while her husband played the electronic keyboard. My friend's deaf brother played the guitar. Deaf brother, you ask? Was that possible? Well, yes, it was, as long as he could feel the beat of the music!

You see…my friend's brother had once been able to hear, had learned to play the guitar, was quite good at it, but then had contracted meningitis. The accompanying high fever of the disease caused him to lose his hearing and he became deaf. At any rate, the deaf brother had learned sign language and belonged to the Deaf Society. The Society was sponsoring a dance for the deaf members and asked if the family of musicians would play for their dance. The main requirement for a successful dance was that all the musicians had to keep time to the music with their feet! The harder they kept time with their feet the stronger the vibrations and the better the deaf people danced!

The deaf people often shouted, "Louder! Louder!" And, so the foot stomping increased. Again, the shout came, "Louder! Louder!"…until the strings started popping on the guitar and the ukulele! One by one they popped until each had only one string left!

Then, before long, even that string broke! Nevertheless, it didn't matter. No one even noticed as long as the foot stomping continued. And, so the musicians stomped even harder. The beat was there, the people could feel it, everyone was happy and the dance was a tremendous success!

Just as there are many kinds of music, there are many kinds of *Christian* music. I think the Lord God Almighty likes them all! Nevertheless, someday, in heaven, it will be made clear if He has a favorite! Currently, I happen to think that as long as the music comes from the person's heart and the person is sincere in their performance of the music...He likes them all!

As a young child, I accompanied my parents to the Y.M.C.A. Camp near Estes Park, Colorado, every summer. One of our favorite Sunday evening activities was to go down to the Administration Building after supper, find ourselves three of the big, old wooden rocking chairs and sit on the porch listening to the hymn sing inside as we watched the day end and the mountains become silhouetted against the evening sky. Somehow, in that setting, those old hymns and the people singing them sounded like music "just this side of heaven."

When I got older and became an employee for three summers during my college years, one of the big conferences at the Camp was a group of Christian athletes. Men and boys came from all over the country for a week of meetings and sporting events.

Each evening after I'd get off work, I'd steal into the back of the chapel hall to listen in on their meetings. When the meeting began, they'd have a time of singing and I would stand there transfixed as 500 male voices sang hymns like that powerful Christian hymn, *"How Great Thou Art!"* Again, it was a sound "just this side of heaven!" And, even to this day, whenever I hear that hymn my memories jettison me back to that chapel hall and those 500 male voices singing praises to God!

In the Bible, we're told, in Psalm 66:1-2, *"Make a joyful noise to God, all the earth; sing the glory of his name; give to him glorious praise!"*

In Psalm 47:1, we read, *"Clap your hands, all ye peoples! Shout to God with loud songs of joy!"*

In Psalm 68:4, *"Sing to God, sing praises to his name, lift up a song to him who rides upon the clouds; his name is the Lord, exult before him!"*

And, in Psalm 97:5-6, *"Sing praises to the Lord with the lyre, with the lyre and the sound of melody! With trumpets and the sound of the horn make a joyful noise before the King, the Lord!"*

The Psalms of the Old Testament contain many verses such as those stated above because they were meant to be sung by the people when accompanied by musical instruments. Aptly named, the word "psalm" meant sacred song or poem. Credited with having written most of the 150 Psalms in the Bible, it's clear that David loved music and offered it up in worship to his God! Indeed, the longest book in the Bible, Psalms could be studied as a separate subject since there's so much that could be learned from them. For the people of Israel in the Old Testament, the Book of Psalms was their hymn book!

David liked the use of musical instruments and such musical instruments as cymbals, harps, lyres and trumpets (1 Chronicles 15:19-24) were used. In addition, other musical instruments such as the pipe, psaltery or zither, tambourines, and the shophar are mentioned. The shophar, a ram or goat's horn, is still used in synagogues today and is often blown at the beginning of the worship service to signal that the service is starting.

An interesting reference to singing and the use of musical instruments in worship can be found in 1 Chronicles 23:

2-5, where it's recorded, *"David assembled all the leaders of Israel and the priests and Levites. The Levites, thirty years old and upward, were numbered, and the total was thirty-eight thousand men. 'Twenty-four thousand of these,' David said, 'shall have charge of the work in the house of the Lord, six thousand shall be officers and judges, four thousand gatekeepers, and **four thousand shall offer praises to the Lord with the instruments which I have made for praise"** (emphasis added). And in another place, in Ezra 2:65, it says, *"...and they had **two hundred male and female singers"*** (emphasis added). So, indeed, "making a joyful noise to God" was very important to the Israelites of the Old Testament!

Turning to the New Testament, in Colossians 3:16, once again we are encouraged to *"Let the word of Christ dwell in you richly, as you teach and admonish one another in all wisdom, and as **you sing psalms and hymns and spiritual songs with thankfulness in your hearts to God"*** (emphasis added).

And, then, in Revelation 14:1-5, we read of a scene to be played out in the final days when Jesus returns to earth at His Second Coming. He comes back for his redeemed bride (group of followers): *"Then I looked, and lo, on Mount Zion stood the Lamb, and with him a hundred and forty-four thousand who had his name and his Father's name written on their foreheads. And I heard a voice from* *heaven like the sound of many waters and like the sound of harpers playing on their harps, and **they sing a new song before the throne** (emphasis added) and before the four living creatures and before the elders. No one could learn that song except the hundred and forty-four thousand who had been redeemed from the earth. It is these who have not defiled themselves with women, for they are chaste, it is these who follow the Lamb wherever he goes; these have been redeemed from mankind as first fruits for God and the Lamb, and in their mouth no lie was found, for they were spotless."* While some of those verses remain unclear, the overall message is "those who follow Jesus Christ will sing a new song before the throne of God in heaven."

Thus, it's important that a Christian use music to worship the Lord! It pleases Him! The music may be with a musical instrument or with your voice.

It's important to learn hymns and to either play them or sing them around the house, in your car, or wherever you can. It's important to purchase compact discs or cassettes of Christian music and play them often, incorporating Christian music into your everyday life. Gradually, you'll find that those melodies, songs and hymns become a part of your inner peace and contentment. For me, I guess even my subconscious likes that music because I often wake up in the morning with the hymns and music running through my head. I start the day with a song to the Lord on my mind and in my heart! Undoubtedly, it will work the same for you, dear reader.

Prayer:
Oh, Lord, help me to make a joyful noise of music and singing before You each day. Help me to strive to always have a song to You in my heart and the words of a song on my lips. Help me to offer up to You a song of love and thanksgiving for all that You do for me each and every day. Help me to praise You throughout my days and to look forward to hearing the ethereal music of the angels and all of the saints down through the ages…all singing praises unto You, O God, as You're seated upon Your throne in heaven!

Amen.

Holy Hands

Two hands and ten fingers…do you know that you have twenty-seven bones in your hands and wrists? There are eight bones in your wrists, five in the palms of your hands and fourteen bones in your fingers…three for each finger and two for each thumb. In addition to bones, there are veins and arteries, muscles, nerves, and ligaments. Eight of your fingers have the ability of flexing in three different places. Your thumb, however, bends in two places. Besides the fingers and thumb you can notice many lines, mounds and bumps caused by the opening and closing of the hand. Turn the hand over and attached to each finger is a fingernail.

Your hands can be considered your personal trademark. They can tell the world a lot about you…what your profession might be, whether you are a calm or nervous person, what's lacking in your diet…all sorts of things. Science tells us that there are no two hands or fingers alike. No two people have the same fingerprints.

My favorite version of the Bible has sixty-nine verses that refer to "hands"…thirty-six of them in the Old Testament and thirty-three in the New Testament. Clearly, the subject of "hands" is an important one!

In Matthew 19:13-15, we read, *"Then children were brought to him (Jesus) that he might lay his hands on them and pray. The disciples rebuked the people, but Jesus said, 'Let the children come to me, and do not hinder them; for to such belongs the kingdom of heaven.' And he laid his hands on them and went away."* In those verses we see the tenderness of Jesus' hands as he dealt with the children.

In Matthew 8:14-15, Jesus went to Peter's house, *"And when Jesus entered Peter's house, he saw his mother-in-law lying sick with a fever; he touched her hand, and the fever left her, and she rose and served him."*

In Matthew 9:25, in response to a ruler's daughter who'd died, he told the crowd to leave and he went into the house, *"he went in and took her by the hand, and the girl arose."* She arose from the dead at the touch of His hand!

In John 8:6-8, we read about a woman caught in the act of adultery. *"Jesus bent down and wrote with his finger on the ground. And as they (the scribes and Pharisees) continued to ask him (about her), he stood up and said to them, 'Let him who is without sin among you be the first to throw a stone at her.' And once more he bent down and wrote with his finger on the ground. But when they heard it, they went away, one by one..."*

In Acts 19:6, we see that another man, Paul, laid his hands on some disciples, *"And when Paul had laid his hands upon them, the Holy Spirit came on them; and they spoke with tongues and prophesied."*

In II Timothy 4:15, we read that the elders laid their hands on people… *"Do not neglect the gift that you have, which was given you by prophetic utterance when the elders laid their hands upon you."*

In Revelation 1:17-18, the Apostle John speaks: *"When I saw him, I fell at his feet as though dead. But he laid his right hand upon me, saying, 'Fear not, I am the first and the last, and the living one; I died, and behold I am alive forever more, and I have the keys of Death and Hades."*

In John 20:24-28, we read of the Apostle Thomas' doubt about the death of Jesus. *"Now Thomas, one of the twelve, called the Twin, was not with them when Jesus came. So the other disciples told him, 'We have seen the Lord.' But he said to them, 'Unless I see in his hands the print of the nails, and place my finger in the mark of the nails, and place my hand in his side, I will not believe.'*

Eight days later, his disciples were again in the house, and Thomas was with them. The doors were shut, but Jesus came and stood among them, and said, 'Peace be with you.' Then he said to Thomas, 'Put your finger here, and see my hands; and put out your hand, and place it in my side; do not be faithless, but believing.' Thomas answered him, "My Lord and my God!"

In just those eight Scripture references to "hands" Jesus' hands blessed children, healed a woman, raised a young girl from the dead, instructed others, comforted the Apostle John, and reassured Thomas that He was alive and had risen from the dead. Also, in those verses, it's seen that there can be power in the hands of other people, other than Jesus...Paul imparted the Holy Spirit, plus the elders made people aware of their gifts in the Holy Spirit.

Indeed, hands can be *so* important as to be "holy hands!" Jesus' hands were holy hands! But, it's also possible for other people's hands to be holy hands. Two of those verses showed that God worked through Paul's hands as well as the elders' hands to accomplish His purposes. Today, in the twenty-first century, Christian hands can have holy power because God *still* uses them to bless people, heal infirmities and illnesses, instruct, comfort, reassure, plus, even raise people from the dead!

Prayer:
Oh, Lord, thank You for creating our hands in such a way that they allow us to do so many things! Help us to use our hands to do good things in our lives and in the lives

of others. Help us to draw closer to You, Lord Jesus, and to use our hands as a sign of reverence for You and to worship You. Help us to strive for "holy hands" that You can work through them…to accomplish Your purposes!

Amen.

Devotional Reading #4

Masks

Have you ever heard that statement, "You can't tell a book by its cover?" Well, I once knew a woman whose name was "Marilyn," and to look at her you'd say there was nothing unusual about her. She looked like a "normal woman!" But, I have to tell you...she had the funniest things happen to her...they were always happening to her! It was incredible! One time, when I used to go long blade ice skating, Marilyn was there. The long blade club had an organist who played for the skaters and he played fifteen "bands" in an evening. A "band" was usually two songs or pieces of music. Well, anyway, Marilyn was a good skater and the men always asked her to skate with them. She had a "full program" with most of the bands asked for...she was popular! One evening when skates became entangled or something happened, Marilyn and her partner fell down. Instantly and much to the chagrin and embarrassment of poor Marilyn...her wig flew off! Away it went...sliding across the ice!

Now, women know how mortifying it is when your wig flies off! Your hair is all matted down flat against your head and you look just awful! Well, I have to tell you...Marilyn was no exception! And there, probably some twenty feet from her on the ice, sat her wig! It was still rounded and it looked as if someone had lost their head!

But Marilyn, with skates still on her feet and clothes wet from having fallen down on the wet rink, got to her knees, crawled the twenty feet over to that wig...picked it up and plopped it back on her head...even though it was all wet from having swooshed across the wet ice! There she sat for a while, tucking loose strands of her hair under the wig and making all of the necessary adjustments to her image! Meanwhile, everyone watched and, needless to say, I don't think any of us will ever forget the day that Marilyn lost her wig at the skating rink!

One other time, Marilyn was driving her car on the freeway. There was a pickup truck ahead of her carrying a mattress. Suddenly, the mattress flew off the truck, landed on the freeway, Marilyn hit it, and it got stuck underneath her car!

She managed to get the car and the mattress over to the side of the road where she got out and tried to dislodge it from under her car. No luck! It was really stuck! Other people stopped to help her and they couldn't budge it, either.

Finally, it became obvious that an expert would have to be contacted. Someone with a tow truck would have to be called as he could hoist the car up enough so that the mattress could be yanked free.

Now, I have to tell you…the towing company thought poor Marilyn was absolutely crazy when she told them that she had a mattress stuck under her car and could they please come and dislodge it? The tow truck driver asked, "You've got *what* stuck under your car? *A mattress*? Say, lady…have you been drinking or are you just plain crazy?"

Well, sad to say, over the years, unfortunately, I've lost track of Marilyn and I sure wonder what's become of her! It's funny how goofy things happen to some people and not to others. Like Marilyn…she looked perfectly normal, but there were always funny things happening to her.

You know, when you look at people it's almost impossible to know what they're like inside or to know what kind of people they are. It's almost as though we go around wearing "masks" that hide our true identities.

Once, for a program at my church, I became a clown. The make-up I put on my face gave me two big round red spots on my cheeks. I added a round red spongy ball to my nose and with a green curly wig, I topped it all off with a pair of Charlie Chaplin round rimmed black glasses. Completing my "ensemble" I wore a red…well, what was that…a red oversized drum majorette's "frock" and topped it all off with a big long green and white dotted tie that came down to my knees. I thought "my mask" and my costume looked pretty funny.

Now, clowns put on make-up and dress up goofy for a number of reasons. First, it helps them hide their own character and identity. Second, it helps them portray someone or something else. Third, it makes people laugh.

In my case, along with giving out lollypops to the kids as I walked along, I'd put that clown "mask and outfit" on for all three of those reasons.

Many people put on "masks," thinking that they can fool other people around them. Those "false fronts," they think, hide their true character and identity and maybe to some extent, on some occasions, those people are right. Maybe they do fool others. But, the sad and hard fact is that no one can hide from themself!

What's inside each of us, what we're really like, what we're made of, our standards, our ideals, our beliefs, our enjoyments, our interests, our good qualities and our not-so-good qualities…those are the important things!
As this devotional reading ends, join me in praying this prayer:

Prayer:
Oh, Lord, teach me to live my life in such a way that I never have to, nor want to, hide behind a mask. Teach me to be honest with myself and all people that I come in contact with. Help me to remember the Golden Rule of doing (good) unto others as they would do (good) unto me. Help me to accept my fellow man as I find him. Help me to be tolerant of others, to be respectful of others, and helpful *to* others. Help me to be less concerned about myself and how I'm perceived by others and to be more concerned about others. Help me to be less self centered and more "other people centered." Help me to be more of a listener to others than a talker about myself. Nevertheless, help me to always be myself, my *natural self,* at all times.

Amen.

Seeds...Perishable or Imperishable

The first time my husband ever planted a garden he didn't know what he was doing. He took some seed packets, found a spot in our backyard that had nothing growing in it, tore open the seed packets and scattered those seeds. He called it his "surprise garden"...if anything came up it would be a surprise! Well, I have to tell you, he got a couple of scrawny radishes, but that was about it! So much for his surprise garden!

I'm afraid I didn't know much more than that when I planted my first "flat" of tomatoes (a "flat"...that's garden talk for several plants all more or less growing together that you buy from the garden nursery). Well, anyway, I dug about six little...what...ditches, holes...and wrapped each clump of tomato roots in newspaper and put them into the ground. I didn't have a clue why that was necessary, but I'd seen my neighbor do that when she planted her tomatoes and her father had owned a garden nursery business so I figured she knew what she was doing. In about two to three weeks the plants looked pretty good and since I'd bought somewhat mature plants, they began to blossom. Once that happened, every day when I came home from work, I'd check out my tomato plants.

Well, my neighbor watched me do that every day and so one day, while I was away at work, she bought some little cherry tomatoes that still had the stems on them and she tied a bunch of them, individually, to my tomato bushes. I have to tell you, I about went crazy with excitement when I saw that...I had tomatoes! And *lots* of them! My garden was a success!

But, then my neighbor came out of her house laughing her head off and so I knew what was going on!

In the Bible, Jesus told a parable about sowing seeds. In Matthew 13:24-30, it says, *"The kingdom of heaven may be compared to a man who sowed good seed in his field; but while men were sleeping, his enemy came and sowed weeds among the wheat, and went away. So when the plants came up and bore grain, then the weeds appeared also. And the servants of the householder came and said to him, 'Sir, did you not sow good seed in your field? How then has it weeds?' He said to them 'An enemy has done this.' The servants said to him, 'Then do you want us to go and gather them?' But he said, 'No; lest in gathering the weeds you root up the wheat along with them. Let both grow together until the harvest; and at harvest time I will tell the reapers, gather the weeds first and bind them in bundles to be burned, but gather the wheat into my barn.'"*

And, in Matthew 13:31-32, it says, *"Another parable he put before them, saying, 'The kingdom of heaven is like a grain of mustard seed which a man took and sowed in his field; it is the smallest of all seeds, but when it has grown it is the greatest of shrubs and becomes a tree, so that the birds of the air come and make nests in its branches.'"*

And, finally, in Matthew 13:36-43, we read that the disciples asked Him to explain the parable of the weeds of the field and He answered them thusly: *"He who sows the good seed is the Son of man; the field is the world, and the good seed means the sons of the kingdom; the weeds are the sons of the evil one, and the enemy who sowed them is the devil; the harvest is the close of the age, and the reapers are angels. Just as the weeds are gathered and burned with fire, so will it be at the close of the age. The Son of man will send his angels, and they will gather out of his kingdom all causes of sin and all evildoers, and throw them into the furnace of fire; there men will weep and gnash their teeth. Then the righteous will shine like the sun in the kingdom of their Father. He who has ears, let him hear."*

And so, we can learn something from those parables. We can substitute ourselves for those seeds. Pretend for a moment that you are a small boy and you have been getting into fights with other boys quite often. Your father and mother are concerned about you and your father says to you, "My son, your mother and I have tried to bring you up right (i.e., planted right seeds). We've worked hard to plant in you seeds of moral decency, respect for the other person, friendliness and kindness to others and to teach you right from wrong. Nevertheless, we think that maybe the good seeds we've worked hard to plant in you have developed into something else without your realizing it (i.e., weeds have developed). We think that's why you're getting into those fights all of the time!"

Once in a while I sit back and "take stock of my life." I take a look at the things I've done recently, the things I've said, and the things I'm involved with to see if there are weeds that need to be gotten rid of or if there's something that needs to be changed. And what about you, dear reader? Have weeds sprung up in your life that are causing you trouble? Have you developed habits that are causing you problems? Do you need to "weed your garden" and root out the troublemakers? Do you need to change your lifestyle in some way?

Regardless of who you are, or what your circumstances are, every one of us could do a little "weeding" from time to time. We could get rid of some things in our lives that probably shouldn't be there. Periodic weeding will help us have a happier and a better life! We need to allow the "good seeds" in ourselves to grow and mature. We need to be sure the good seeds are watered and nurtured so that we live lives pleasing to God and to those around us.

Prayer:
Oh, Lord, help me to review my life today and to be aware of what I'm doing that I shouldn't be doing. Help me to review how I'm behaving in different situations, and if there are situations that I've not handled right, help me to make better choices next time. Help me to review what I've said to others recently and if I've said things badly or shouldn't have said them at all, help me to do better next time. Reveal to me, Lord, those things in my life that shouldn't be there and help me to "weed them out," to get rid of them, that I might be found more acceptable to You. I ask You to forgive me. And, as You are the Son of man who sows good seeds, *help me to be one of Your good seeds*...Your son or daughter who strives to be an example of Your Kingdom here on earth and who will, one day, be welcomed into Your Kingdom above.

Amen

Devotional Reading #6

Dreams

It had been a lifelong dream of mine to see the Matterhorn Mountain near Zermatt, Switzerland. As a kid, I'd seen a movie that centered its story line around that mountain. The scenery in that movie had been magnificent and the story line had tugged at my childhood heartstrings. I dreamed that some day I might be able to go there and see that mountain.

In 1997, John and I flew to Frankfurt, Germany, gathered up our luggage and took the train southward about one hundred miles to a small village where our German friends lived. Together, we were going to travel by car to Switzerland. Yes, you guessed it...our destination...the Matterhorn!

Our German friends had not been there before and made it plain that "this trip was being made as a kindly gesture to me" as there were other places they would have preferred to visit with us.

Nevertheless, after driving as far as we could with the car, and then taking a train, we finally reached Zermatt! We checked into our hotel and all four of us had to admit that the mountain was a splendid sight as it loomed magnificently above! So, on the following day we bought our tickets and were soon on board a "cog train" ascending up a nearby mountain. (A cog train has a set of gears that grip another set of gears in the ground so that the train doesn't suddenly go whizzing out of control back down the mountain!) The day had dawned sunny and bright, and all four of us were eager for a sightseeing adventure.

Gradually, we passed the timber line and ultimately came to the chalet at the end of the trip. And there it was…an adjacent peak…the Matterhorn!

Well, I have to tell you…words simply *can't* tell you what a breathtaking sight that mountain was! It was even *more* awesome a spectacle seeing it in person than any photo I'd ever seen of it! Absolutely incredible! So magnificent! So beautiful!

And as we sat on the chalet's deck facing that awesome mountain, I couldn't believe that a life-time dream of mine had, that day, come true!

In *Webster's Dictionary*, the word "dream" has many meanings. In the story above, the word "dream" referred to a fond hope or aspiration that was fulfilled when I saw the Matterhorn Mountain. A "dream" could also refer to a fanciful vision of the conscious mind as in a "daydream." Then again, a "dream" might refer to someone lovely or charming, as "she was a dream!" But, perhaps the commonest use of the word "dream" refers to a sequence of images, thoughts, or sensations passing through a sleeping person's mind.

In the Bible, there are many references to "dreams." In the Old Testament, in Genesis 20:3-7, God appeared in a dream to Abimelech, king of Gerar, regarding a wrong he had committed. Abimelech had taken Sarah, the wife of Abraham, because Abraham had told him Sarah was his sister. Sarah, likewise, had said that Abraham was her brother. But, before Sarah's integrity was violated, God said to Abimelech in the dream that if he restored Sarah to Abraham, no harm would befall him. And, because Abimelech did restore Sarah to Abraham, Abimelech's own wife and female slaves could, once again, bear children. God rewarded Abimelech and his household.

In Genesis 37:5-19, Joseph had a dream and in it he dreamed that the sun, the moon, and eleven stars were bowing down to him. Joseph's brothers interpreted the dream to mean that they would have to bow down to Joseph, so they conspired to kill him. They threw him in a pit until some Midianite traders approached, then they drew him out of the pit and sold him to the Midianites.

The traders took him to Egypt. Meanwhile, Joseph's brothers had taken Joseph's robe, killed a goat, dipped his robe in its blood, and given the robe to Joseph's father as proof that Joseph was dead. You will have to read the rest of the story for yourself, but suffice it to say that all this trouble began because of a "dream."

In 1 Kings 3:5, another man, Solomon, had a dream in which God appeared to him. And, in Daniel 2:1-49, King Nebuchadnezzar had a dream in which God appeared to him. The King summoned his magicians, enchanters, sorcerers and the Chaldeans (who believed in astrology and the occult) to try and interpret his dream and tell him what it meant. None of them proved successful in telling him what the dream meant. Ultimately, of course, the King summoned Daniel to interpret the dream and he was able to do it.

In the New Testament, in Matthew 1:20-23, an angel of the Lord appeared, in a dream, to Joseph, the son of David, betrothed to Mary, and said, *"Joseph, son of David, do not fear to take Mary your wife, for that which is conceived in her is of the Holy Spirit; she will bear a son, and you shall call his name Jesus, for he will save his people from their sins."*

And later, (Matthew 2: 12-13), Joseph was warned in a dream not to return to the land of Herod, but to depart to their own country by another way. An angel of the Lord told Joseph, *"Arise, take the child and his mother, and flee to Egypt, and remain there till I tell you; for Herod is about to search for the child, to destroy him."*

And, finally, in Acts 2:17-21, it says: *"And in the last days it shall be, God declares, that I will pour out my Spirit upon all flesh, **and your sons and your daughters shall prophesy, and your young men shall see visions, and your old men shall dream dreams;** (emphasis added) yea, and on my menservants and my maidservants in those days I will pour out my Spirit; and they shall prophesy. And I will show wonders in the heavens above and signs on the earth beneath, blood, and fire, and vapor of smoke; the sun shall be turned into darkness and the moon into blood, before the day of the Lord comes, the great and manifest day. And it shall be that whoever calls on the name of the Lord shall be saved."*

Thus, we see that "dreams" run the gamut…from merely "hopes" we have for future events, to "day dreams" in which our mind wanders to another time, place, or event, to thinking lovely thoughts about someone (i.e., she's a "dream"), to actually dreaming dreams in the course of sleeping at night.

All of those kinds of dreams have a purpose in our lives. Nevertheless, as it says in Philippians 4:8-9, *"Whatever is true, whatever is honorable, whatever is just, whatever is pure, whatever is lovely, whatever is gracious, if there is any excellence, if there is anything worthy of praise, think about these things...and the God of peace will be with you."*

Dear Reader, strive to have "good dreams"...whichever kind of dream you're referring to!

Prayer:
Oh, Lord, help me to seek after good dreams, dreams that will give me peace of mind and a joy in living! In my waking state, help me to fill my mind with good and wholesome thoughts and activities so that at night when dreams come, they are peaceful, good dreams. Help me to seek after You, Lord, and to be ever mindful that You still speak to people...and sometimes it may be in the dreams we dream.

Amen.

Devotional Reading #7

Clouds

Flying back to Minnesota from a Christian conference I'd attended in New Orleans, LA, the airplane climbed higher to rise above the thunder and lightning of a rainstorm. Looking out the window, suddenly the sky was clear again and then, oh, my, it took my breath away…the sky was a bright golden yellow amidst shades of sunset orange as the billows of white thunderhead clouds reflected vibrant rays of sunlight! I think the pilot was left breathless too, as I felt him bank and curve the plane around the billowing thunderheads, allowing passengers on both sides of the plane to see the spectacular sight. It was an awesome scene I'll never forget!

From the time I was a child, my father had instilled in me an appreciation for rainstorms. Sometimes he'd come and get me out of bed and take me to a window so we could watch the storm together. He wanted to make sure that I never feared rainstorms with their accompanying thunder and lightning. We'd often sit by the window and watch the storm clouds gather. Some of them would be swirling about as though someone with a huge paddle in his hands was mixing them up. Others, on the contrary, would be marching forward like a mighty wall. Then, shafts of lightning would play tag with each other as they flashed in and out of the clouds. And, each rapier-like thrust of lightning was followed by a protesting snarl of thunder that shook the earth and made the window rattle. Dad and I loved to watch such aerial displays of power and might!

You know, dear reader, people can sometimes be likened to clouds. Some people go about their lives angry, grumbling and complaining a lot of the time. Those people often cause thunderbolts of division and dissension in their wake.

Then, there are people who, like lazy, drifting clouds, never seem to contribute much or go anywhere. The world is filled with lazy, indifferent individuals who drift and float from one thing to another, working and carrying their share of responsibility only long enough to satisfy their own needs.

In between those two extremes are those beautiful, serene people who, like such clouds, sail through life as though they had a definite purpose and someplace wonderful to go. Their outline is sharp and clear cut and it appears that they have a sense of determination as they hurry on their way. There are, on earth, people who are like those beautiful serene clouds and they're a pleasure to know. Where do you stand, dear reader? If people could be divided into the three simple groups of clouds given above, which group would you fit into? Which type of cloud group best illustrates your personality? Are you the kind of person who's always in a turmoil? Or, are you, perhaps, the laid back drifting kind of person? Or, are you like that third group...the type of person that has a quiet serene determination and a definite purpose?

God has placed each of us here on earth to do certain tasks. He's given us individual unique abilities and talents that he wants us to use to get those specific tasks done. It's as if God created us to do those tasks! Yet, there are many people who fail to realize that they should make the most of every opportunity along life's way to prepare themselves for the tasks that lie ahead. Many people never seem to realize that they have a responsibility to God...and their fellow human beings...to perform their tasks, whatever they are, and to do them to the best of their abilities!

I think that the words of the following poem (taken from a book my father wrote) are words that should be heeded and taken to heart. The poem is titled, "Do it Now."

If you have hard work to do, do it now,
Today the skies are clear and blue,
Tomorrow clouds may come in view,
Yesterday is not for you; do it now.

If you have a song to sing, sing it now,
Let the tones of gladness ring,
Clear as song of birds in spring,
Let each day some music bring; sing it now.

If you have kind words to say, say them now,
Tomorrow may not come your way,
Do a kindness while you may,
Loved ones will not always stay; say them now.

If you have a smile to show, show it now,
Make hearts happy, roses grow,
Let the friends around you know,
The love you have before they go, show it now.

Thus, dear reader, while simplistically speaking, people may be likened to the three types of clouds…and you can think about which type of cloud group you seem to belong in, let us move on with this devotional reading and see what the Bible has to say about the subject of "clouds."

In the Old Testament, in Psalm 78:13-14, we read about how God dealt with the Israelites, *"He divided the sea and let them pass through it, and made the waters stand like a heap. In the daytime he led them with a cloud, and all the night with a fiery light."* And, in Psalm 105:39,

"He spread a cloud for a covering, and a fire to give light by night."

And, in the New Testament, those words are referenced in 1 Corinthians 10:1-9, *"I want you to know, brethren, that our fathers were all under the cloud, and all passed through the sea, and all were baptized into Moses in the cloud and in the sea, and all ate the same supernatural food and all drank the same supernatural drink. For they drank from the supernatural Rock which followed them, and that Rock was Christ."*

Thus, we see that God, the Father, often covered over the people of Israel and led them by means of a cloud. We also see that Jesus Christ was an intrinsic part of that picture, but the Israelites didn't know it.

And then, in Matthew 17:5-8, we read that while Peter was talking with Jesus, *"...lo, a bright cloud overshadowed them, and a voice from the cloud said, 'This is my beloved Son, with whom I am well pleased; listen to him.' When the disciples heard this, they fell on their faces, and were filled with awe. But Jesus came and touched them, saying, 'Rise, and have no fear.' And when they lifted up their eyes, they saw no one but Jesus only."* Thus, God, the Father, spoke from within an overshadowing bright cloud and told the disciples that Jesus was His beloved Son and that they should listen to Him.

In Matthew 24:30-31, it tells us that one day Jesus, God's beloved Son, will come back to earth within a cloud. *"...then will appear the sign of the Son of man in heaven, and then all the tribes of the earth will mourn, and they will see the Son of man coming on the clouds of heaven with power and great glory; and he will send out his angels with a loud trumpet call, and they will gather his elect from the four winds, from one end of heaven to the other."* And, again, in Revelation 1:7, *"Behold, he is coming with the clouds, and every eye will see him, every one who pierced him; and all tribes of the earth will wail on account of him. Even so. Amen."*

And, lastly, in I Thessalonians 4:15-17, we read, *"...we who are alive, who are left until the coming of the Lord, shall not precede those who have fallen asleep. For the Lord himself will descend from heaven with a cry of command, with the archangel's call, and with the sound of the trumpet of God. **And the dead in Christ will rise first; then we who are alive, who are left, shall be caught up together with them in the clouds** (emphasis added) to meet the Lord in the air; and so we shall always be with the Lord."*

Dear reader, at the close of the age, when Christ returns to earth, what spectacular clouds will accompany and surround Him! Can you speculate on what that scene will be like? And, can you speculate on what it will be like to see the graves crack open and the dead in Christ rise to meet Him in the clouds, followed by those who are still alive?

Prayer:
Oh, Lord, help me this day to frequently think about that scene I've just speculated upon…the scene when You, Jesus, will return to earth amidst the clouds. Help me to grow spiritually until that day. Help me to do the tasks set before me to the best of my abilities and talents. Help me to be mindful of my fellow human beings, to always treat them kindly and with love and respect. Help me to love You, Jesus, more and more with each passing day so that I will be ready for that day when I will be among the chosen elect who rise to meet You in the clouds!

Amen

Amongst Weeds of Disappointment

With great anticipation and excitement, I'd arrived at the lake where, in the summer time, my parents and I had visited my aunt and uncle. Richer than we were, they had a lake cabin! Now, however, the cabin was locked up for the winter; the day was cloudy and crisp with a slight breeze blowing, and the temperature was, well, tolerably cold. It was, after all, Minnesota, and I'd come to the lake to ice fish. For me, that lake in the winter time was a whole new scene…a whole new ball game, so to speak. Nevertheless, eagerly I unloaded my gear from the car and toted it all out onto the lake. I expected great fun and I had the afternoon ahead of me!

I took my four foot chisel and, scraping away the foot of snow that had fallen, I began to chop a six inch round hole in the ice. Around and around I moved, chopping in a circle, then stopping to scoop out the ice chips before chopping some more. Off came the jacket! More chipping, more chopping! Whew…I was drenched in sweat! But, finally, when my arm disappeared up to the elbow scooping out ice chips, I could tell water was close by. And then…swoosh! With one more mighty chop the water rushed in and filled the hole. A little more chopping so that the bottom of the hole felt rounded and I grabbed the wire scoop to clean out the last of the ice chips. Ah, sweet success!

But, hello! Hey! What's this? What's in the middle of the hole? Oh, my gosh! It's a gigantic weed…growing smack dab in the middle of that hole I'd just cut! Ohhhhh, noooooo! Groan!

"OK, that's life, don't be daunted!" I said. "Move farther out onto the lake and begin the whole process all over again! Chop another hole!"

So, when all was said and done and no weed appeared in the next hole, I hastily got my fishing pole, line, bobber, sinker, and hook ready. Even though my hands were freezing from the icy water in the minnow bucket and from baiting the hook, I took that minnow, spit on him for "good luck" and dropped him into the hole. Now let the fishing begin!

Of course, a good fisherman rarely is content to watch just one pole…so I took my chisel, walked a little ways away and began chopping yet another hole. Once again, around and around in a circle I went with my chisel! Then, with a little more than one-fourth of it finished, I looked over at the other hole just in time to see my fishing pole being pulled across the ice…and it was headed straight for the open hole! Ohhhhhh noooo! Sheesh! I made a mad dash and lunged for that pole with every ounce of strength I had left! Alas, I wasn't swift enough! All was in vain as the entire pole, bobber, hook, line and sinker disappeared down the hole! A big Northern fish had gone off with the entire thing!

Well, I have to tell you, that pretty much ended my enthusiasm for "ice fishing" that day! I was "spent!" I had no more energy nor ambition for that day's fishing adventure! The idea of going to the grocery store and buying a nice fresh fish appealed *very* much. Thus, off I went! So much for ice fishing that day!

Dear reader, you know many times the "weeds of disappointment" come into our lives. Things don't always turn out the way we expect them to or the way we hope they will. In the Bible, there was the wedding at Cana whereby the wine for the celebration ran out, and I'm sure the parents of the wedding couple were very disappointed. Jesus' mother saw that and she asked Jesus if He could help. Even though His time of ministry had not yet come, because He honored and respected His mother, He told the servants to fill six stone jars with water, each holding twenty or thirty gallons. When they were filled to the brim, Jesus said, *"Now draw some out, and take it to the steward of the feast."* *So they took it.* (John 2:8)

In that example, Jesus "came to the rescue and saved the day" for the wedding celebration. He turned the water into wine…the *best* wine at that wedding celebration! As we read in John 2:10, "Every man serves the good wine first; and when men have drunk freely, then the poor wine, but you have kept the good wine until now." This was the first of many things Jesus did in His ministry.

During another time in the Bible, a man had been ill for 38 years and had lain by the side of the Pool of Bethesda. He, like many others, believed that whenever the angel of the Lord came down at certain times and troubled the water, whoever stepped in first after the troubling of the water was healed of their diseases. Disappointment had bothered the man for many years as he had no one to help him into the pool at that moment. Someone else always benefited from the healing. Nevertheless, Jesus came along and said to him, *"Rise, take up your pallet, and walk."* And at once the man was healed and he took up his pallet and walked. (John 5:2-9)

Many are the times when disappointments come into our lives…the weed in the middle of my ice fishing hole, the disappearance of the whole fishing pole in yet another fishing hole, and the two examples from the Bible. The disappointment I had of not being able to catch a fish was solved simply by going to the store and buying a fish. It was an easy solution to the problem. But, in the other two examples, and indeed, in *many* of the examples we can think of in our lives...we must look to someone else for the solution. Often times that someone else must be the Lord Jesus Christ, as He's the only one with power enough to help us!

Prayer:
Oh, Lord Jesus, help us not to get caught up nor tangled in the "weeds of disappointment"...weeds that can cause us to "give up and become disheartened." Help us to solve the problems we're able to solve, but for those we need help with... help us to look to You, Jesus, for that help!

Amen

Devotional Reading #9

By Wisdom a House Is Built

Proverbs 22:6 says: *"Train up a child in the way he should go and when he is old he will not depart from it."*

I used to love to go trout fishing with my dad in the Black Hills of South Dakota. When my dad had been a kid of about twelve, his father had taken him along while he worked in a saw mill near a small town called "Mystic." Tucked "way back in the hills," Mystic had, as the saying goes, a small river that ran through it. And, every summer when I was growing up, on our way to Colorado, we'd have to stop in Mystic and trout fish. Mystic was one of those unique spots that, over the decades, hadn't changed much. In fact, the buildings were the same ones that had been there when dad was a boy and if anything, were less in number. The stream was a small one, and unless you were "a native to the area" you'd probably figure it too small to contain any fish. Nevertheless, Dad and I knew better! Dad would put his hanky around his neck under his cap, roll down his long sleeves to guard against the hoards of ferocious gnats that suddenly appeared; I'd do the same, and away we'd go to catch those elusive trout.

We'd always get at least a couple of nice-sized trout which we'd clean on the spot before we left, take them back to the motel room and fry 'em up for supper! Great eating!

One day, however, Dad wanted to hike over the hills to an even more secluded stream he'd remembered from his youth. The morning dawned bright and sunny and as we prepared to leave our motel room dad told me to drink a couple of glasses of water. He said I'd need the moisture for the hike and hill climb. Nevertheless, since it was a chilly morning and I wasn't at all thirsty I refused. He insisted, but I remained adamant.

So, our day, our hike and our adventure began. We hiked and climbed and hiked some more! Finally, around noon-time, we arrived at the secluded stream he'd remembered from his youth. There was an old miner's tumbled down shack back there and nothing else. The area had remained as it was in Dad's youth.

By that time, however, with all that hiking and climbing, I was thirsty. Dad said to drink from the stream, but to only swish the water around in my mouth, not swallow it. Dad said, "Don't drink it because we don't know if it's safe. We don't know if drinking it will make you sick because of where it comes from or what's been dumped into it." Oh, how I ached for a good cold drink! We tried our luck in that secluded stream, but no trout were there.

The stream seemed void of fish altogether. (Maybe it was a good thing that I hadn't swallowed any of the water!) What a disappointment! Thus, back we trudged, over hill and dale again, back to where we had begun our trek.

By the time we were back in our car heading toward the motel I "could spit cotton," my mouth was so dry. I wished I'd taken my father's advice and drank those two full glasses of water earlier that day!

Back in Mystic, dad filled up the gas tank at the local filling station while I went inside to buy a cold bottle of grape pop. I chug-a-lugged that bottle down in one gulp and bought another one! Meanwhile, watching me, Dad warned me not to drink that cold drink too fast or I'd get stomach cramps. Again, I didn't listen to him, and yup, that's what happened! I got a stomach cramp so badly I thought I was going to die right there on the spot! It hurt something terrible!

So, kid that I was, I learned a couple of valuable lessons that day. I also learned that good parents generally know what's best for their kids!

My husband's father never taught him much about fishing. In fact, I don't recall ever hearing about John going fishing with his father. Consequently, by the time I married him, John hadn't developed an interest in fishing.

Going fishing was not on his list of enjoyable things to do. He couldn't have cared less about it. Now, you'd have to know my husband to understand that he was a very merciful person, a very kind-hearted person, a person who always felt sorry for the "under-dog," he was someone who was able to "put himself in the other person's shoes." He could identify with the other person. He could feel what the other person felt. So, I guess it was just natural that his merciful nature caused him to feel sorry for a fish that was caught! He even felt sorry for the minnow!

Nevertheless, once in the early days of our marriage, I took him fishing, and after fishing along the bank of the lake I looked up to see him walking toward me carrying his pole and attached to the line was…well, what *was* that, anyway? What was that thing? From a distance, it didn't look like a fish and I yelled, "Hey, John, what did you catch there? What is that thing?"

And, there, clamped onto the end of his fishing line, just as tight as it could clamp was, of all things, a clam! He'd caught a clam! And, so, right then and there I could see that fishing was not for him! It definitely was not going to be within his list of better achievements nor desirable activities!

In Proverbs 24:3-4, we read, *"By wisdom a house is built, and by understanding it is established; by knowledge the rooms are filled with all precious and pleasant riches."*

For me, those precious and pleasant days of being with my dad while fishing have become rich, priceless memories.

And, as a kid, while I hadn't read Proverbs 19:20, I should have and heeded its message. *"Listen to advice and accept instruction, that you may gain wisdom for the future."*

So it is with our heavenly Father. We ought to strive to hear His leadings, promptings, and teachings in our lives because He loves us *far more* than our earthly fathers ever did and He's always there...with His eye upon us! Sometimes He allows us to make our own choices and decisions that He knows aren't in our best interests. But He says, "Ok, my child, go ahead, make that mistake...it grieves me, but go ahead and make that mistake. Then, next time you'll know what not to do or what to do differently."

Dear reader...can you recall a time in your life as a child or young person when a parent or another adult advised you about something but you proceeded on your own anyway and the end result wasn't so good because you had failed to listen to the words of wisdom from the older person?

Or was there ever a time in your life when you wished you'd had some prior instructions and guidance from an adult, but hadn't?

Or was there ever a time in your life when you felt that your "inner voice" told you one thing, but you proceeded in another direction and subsequently wished you'd listened to that inner voice?

Again, in Proverbs 4:1-5, we read, *"Hear, O sons, a father's instruction, and be attentive, that you may gain insight; for I give you good precepts; do not forsake my teaching. When I was a son with my father, tender, the only one in the sight of my mother, he taught me, and said to me, 'Let your heart hold fast my words; keep my commandments, and live, do not forget, and do not turn away from the words of my mouth...'"*

Dear reader, if we can just remember those words! And, be they spoken by a good, earthly Father, or by our heavenly Father, they are for our benefit.

Prayer:

Oh, Lord, when I was a child, I spoke like a child, I thought like a child, I reasoned like a child. Help me, oh Lord, to realize that by wisdom a house is built and that when I was young (a young "house," really) my earthly father influenced my actions and behaviors. Many times the wisdom I received from him was good and for my benefit. But now, as I grow older, *Your* wisdom is what I need to seek. I need to listen to the wisdom that You often impart to me through that "still, small voice" that's inside of me...the still small voice that directs me along a right pathway in life. O Lord, please help that still small voice within me to become louder and clearer so that I don't miss the wisdom of what You're trying to say to me or teach me. Help me to spend time with You each day, praying to You, praising You, studying Your Words in the Bible, incorporating those Words into my life, and listening for Your voice. But, help me, O Lord, to maintain a "childlike faith in You" that trusts You completely and does not seek wisdom for wisdom's sake. Help me to seek understanding in the important things in life...so that ultimately the rooms of my life will be filled with the knowledge of "precious and pleasant riches" and that, ultimately, I'll be with You in eternity!

Amen

Devotional Reading #10

Summer Camp

In the Old Testament, in Numbers 2, *"The Lord said to Moses and Aaron, 'The people of Israel shall encamp each by his own standard, with the ensigns of their father's houses; they shall encamp facing the tent of meeting on every side.'"* In that chapter of Numbers it's laid out where each of the tribes of Israel shall camp. For example, "Those to encamp on the east side toward the sunrise shall be of the standard of the camp of Judah by their companies." Then, it goes on to say, "Those to encamp next to him shall be the tribe of Issachar," and so on through the placement of all the tribes.

Then, in Numbers 33, the journey of the people of Israel to the land of Canaan is told about and where their encampments were to be along the route. It says, in Numbers 33:2, *"Moses wrote down their starting places, stage by stage, by command of the Lord; and these are their stages according to their starting places."* In verses 5-7, we read, *"So the people of Israel set out from Rameses and encamped at Succoth. And they set out from Succoth, and encamped at Etham, which is on the edge of the wilderness. And they set out from Etham, and turned back to Pihahiroth, which is east of Baalzephon; and they encamped before Migdol,"* and so on. Of course, we know that the Israelites, because of their rebellion and disobedience to God, wandered through the wilderness for 40 years, encamping at various places.

How very different those encampments were from the places we call "camps" today. Yet, in 20th and 21st Century America, going to camp in the summer is still an interesting event. Dear reader, have you ever been to summer camp? Or have you ever had a friend or were the parent of a child who went and subsequently shared their experiences with you?

There is still much that can be learned from a trip to summer camp! My father worked for the Y.M.C.A. for 35 years of his life and because of that, I grew up being the only girl at the boy's two week summer camp. Dad was the camp director and mom helped in the kitchen with the meals, and since I was an only child, I was alone a lot. My parents were busy and I had to pretty much amuse myself the best way I could all day.

During afternoon swim times I tried to avoid walking from our cabin past the boy's dormitories on my way to the kitchen and mess hall because the boys would yell out at me. "Hey, Susie, come here and see what I've got!" Now, I was only ten or eleven years old at the time, uninterested in boys as yet and I certainly didn't care to see what it was that they wanted to show me. I had better things to do with my time!

One of those years I can remember that I had a brand new two-piece bathing suit. I was one of those gals who "matured early," was a woman by age twelve, and so by the age of ten or eleven…was well on my way to "shaping up." Well, as the proud owner of a brand new two piece bathing suit, my dad said it would be all right if I accompanied him into the lake during the swimming time with the boys. I was all excited, and so I went.

Dad had taught me how to swim when I was only five years old and he'd taught me how to do so by having me lie on my stomach on the piano bench in our living room. He taught me how to kick my legs and to be sure and keep my knees stiff. Then, he taught me how to move my arms in the crawl stroke. Lastly, he taught me how to take a breath to the side when my arm was extended up over my head. So, by the time I got into the swimming pool at the Y.M.C.A. on family night, I pretty much knew how to swim. I'd been taught the fundamentals!

Back to the day of the brand new swimming suit. The boys were in swimming all around me, but I had no time for them. Rather, the refreshing coolness of the water on a perfect summer day, just right for lake swimming, had me too busy splashing, kicking around and swimming! Thus, time passed, until giving a quick look away from supervising the boys, dad yelled over at me, "Hey, honey, how's the new swimming suit holding up?"

In quick response, I gathered my feet under me and immediately jumped about two feet straight out of the water as I yelled back, "Great, Dad! Just great!" Nevertheless...it was then that I realized that the top half of my two piece bathing suit was, at that moment, up around my neck! Oh, no! Groan! One of life's more embarrassing moments, to be sure!

At summer camp, the boys loved to play softball on the ball field right outside the mess hall, but lately the ball field had a serious problem that made for hazardous playing conditions. The camp maintenance men had tried everything to get rid of a pesky mole who'd been tunneling underneath the ball field. They'd tried to smoke him out, drown him out with the hose, and trap him. Nothing had worked. It was dangerous for the boys to play softball there, because stepping into one of the mole's tunneled areas where the ground was soft could result in a sprained ankle or broken leg. Playing softball had been canceled and the boys were unhappy.

I don't know where I'd learned of it, but I'd heard that a mole comes out of his hole at 4:00 p.m. every day. As a kid of about ten years old and not knowing any better, one day I positioned myself on the hill overlooking that mole's hole. Sure enough, at 4:00 p.m. he came out of that hole! I jumped up, ran down the hill, headed for the tool shed, grabbed a shovel, raced back up the hill and hit that mole over the head. I gave that pesky varmint a migraine headache he couldn't forget, and in the ensuing days I think he found himself another home, elsewhere. The ball playing field was rid of him and now the boys could play softball again!

Skit night at camp was always fun for the boys. The camp counselors sang goofy songs together, told jokes, did magic tricks, handed out ice cream bars and, in general, gave the boys a fun evening. One favorite activity, done every year, was "taking individual boy's photos via using a common kitchen spoon." It would never work today, but in those days without today's mass media it was easier to convince twelve year olds that that trick was possible, and so Dad would "talk it up" and convince them that the spoon he was holding was a special spoon, bought at a great price and not sold everywhere.

He'd step up to a young fellow, tell him that the quality of this photo he was about to take was exceptionally good and maybe the lad wanted to think about mailing it home to his parents in his next letter! Then, Dad would address the boy next to the chosen lad and say he hoped that he wasn't too sorry that he had not been chosen for this special honor. Oh, Dad did a great job of hyping up that room full of boys!

Then, with a great deal of fanfare, he'd belabor the taking of the photo. He'd wipe the spoon with his hanky to be sure the lens was clean, he'd shade the spoon so the lighting would be correct. He'd position the young fellow so his best side was enhanced, and finally, he'd take the photo! Then, Dad would move off to the side of the room, saying that the photo needed time to develop. The boys would have to wait to see the results.

Meanwhile, a camp counselor would come into the mess hall and, in a loud voice as he walked up to my Dad, he'd ask, "Hey, Doc, what's going on in here? What are you guys doing?" Dad would say, "Well, we've been taking photos of the guys so they can send them home to their parents. I'm waiting for the photo in this spoon camera to develop." "Spoon camera?" the camp counselor asked, "You can't take a photo of anyone with a spoon!" Dad said, "Yes, you can…here, see the photo of the last guy I just photographed," and he handed the spoon to the counselor.

Meanwhile, it was prearranged that someone else in the room was to sit and move exactly the same way as the person just photographed. The camp counselor knew who that imitator was and so he casually looked at that person and then looked at the boys and ultimately, he'd choose the boy who'd just "had his photo taken." Things proceeded nicely and ultimately the correct boy was picked out of the crowd by the camp counselor. The boys were at a loss to know what had happened and some of them were so impressed that they wanted to know where Dad had purchased that spoon. Where did he get it and where could they get one just like it?

Well, one skit night at summer camp brought me to tears as I watched my father stumble into the mess hall. He was moaning and groaning, convulsing in pain as he clutched his stomach! The camp counselors rushed over to him and helped him climb up onto the counter. Everyone was screaming and yelling and carrying on something terrible! I was scared stiff!

Then, the camp counselors put on hospital gowns and masks and announced that the situation was critical and that they had to operate immediately! (Wow, I almost went crazy!)

They took a big butcher knife from the kitchen and made it look as though they were slicing my dad's guts open! Meanwhile, he was still moaning and groaning and writhing in pain! Suddenly, it looked like he was bleeding profusely as "blood" shot upwards from his body! (Later, they told me it had been nothing more than "red bug juice…the name we used for kool aid!") But, standing there, I about lost it! I was a basket case!

Then, the camp counselors began taking things out of my dad's stomach. All sorts of things! A big steak bone, a huge candy bar, part of a garden hose (undoubtedly, left over from trying to drown out that mole in the ball field!), hamburger hash…everyone's favorite meal…from last night's supper, (ha!). All sorts of things came out of him ending with…a long heavy linked metal chain! By that time the boys in that mess hall were rolling on the floor in laughter! They were jumping up and down and carrying on something awful…and a few of them pointed their fingers at me, his daughter! I didn't know what to make of it all…I was bawling my eyes out because I never knew my dad had so many things inside his gut!

Well, ultimately, they "stitched" dad back up and dad got down off of the counter, came over to me, put his arm around me and said, "Honey, it's ok, it was all a big joke! I'm all right!"

Well, that's life at summer camp! There are many such stories from kids who've been to summer camp!

Of course, there are many different kinds of summer camps, even in 21ˢᵗ century America! Some, besides Y camps, are church camps. And, while I can't speak for all such camps, I think a lot of camps incorporate God into them for the sake of the campers. I think, personally, that camp devotions ought to be incorporated into most summer camps and that devotions might, in fact, be one of the most important aspects of a camper's camp experience.

At the Y.M.C.A. camp that my father was the director for...*devotions were a part of every day.* Beginning in the morning, there was a word of prayer in each cabin as the boys began their day's activities. Then, before meal times...three times that day...at breakfast, lunch, and dinner, there was a prayer said in thanksgiving for the food. And, finally, before bedtime each night, devotions concluded the day.

Dear reader, what about your experiences at summer camp or the camping experiences of a friend or your child? Were there devotions? And, what about you, dear reader? How much of your day is spent in prayer? Think about the words of this prayer as you pray it:

Prayer:
Oh, heavenly Father, help me to remember that the Israelites had to wander 40 years in the wilderness and had to make their encampments at many different

places…all because they were rebellious and disobedient to God. Help me, O Lord, to move ever forward because I look to You for my leadership. Help me not to be rebellious nor disobedient to You. Direct my pathways this day, O Lord. Living life is like being in "boot camp" where each day has its obstacles and challenges. Help me to begin each of my days in prayer with You so that, having dedicated the day into Your care and keeping, whatever the day's obstacles and challenges, they'll come under Your advisement and direction for my life. If necessary, help me to get up just a little earlier so that I might spend time with You at the outset of each new day. Be with me throughout my day, O Lord, and keep me safely in Your care until my evening prayers conclude this day.

Amen

Devotional Reading #11

Out of Step

Have you ever felt, dear reader, that you were "out of step" with those around you…that somehow your thinking or interests differed from those around you? Have you ever felt unusual or maybe even odd when compared to the other people around you? If so, then perhaps you'll be able to relate to the following two stories a little…

As a young girl I used to go down to the Y.M.C.A. where Dad was the Physical Education Director and, with the boys, I'd go down into the window wells around the outside of the building. You see, the Y building was about two, maybe three blocks, from the Mississippi River and sometimes frogs would come up from the River and fall into the window wells. We'd go down into those window wells, get the frogs and have frog races down the hallways of the Y. It was great fun! Once, I was lucky enough to find *two* frogs in the window wells and so, I had *two* frogs jumping when the next race started. Now, that kept me plenty busy, I can tell you!

On one occasion, I thought one of my frogs looked a little sick, like maybe he needed some water or something. So, I put him in the drinking fountain and turned the water on him. I guess that wasn't what he wanted because he jumped behind the water fountain and so I was down on all fours, trying to reach him behind the fountain, when one of the Y men came by and asked, "Little girl, what are you doing?" I looked up at him, very concerned, and said, "I'm trying to get my frog…he jumped behind there when I was trying to give him a drink!" Well, that man looked at me with the *strangest* look and said, "Errrrrrr, ohhhhh, o.k., I see…ahhhhh, *your frog* is behind there," and off he went, mumbling something about how little girls sure had changed since his day and age!

Then one night, on another occasion, Dad had his Y.M.C.A. leader's club of boys come to our house for a meeting. Since I was only five years old or so, Mom and Dad had put me to bed early and I was supposedly asleep. But, as the evening wore on and the meeting progressed, I couldn't sleep. I'd been hearing bits and pieces of the meeting as the boys laughed and discussed things. At one point, whatever it was that they needed to take a vote on I never knew, but I heard my dad say, "Whoever agrees with this, vote 'aye,' whoever doesn't agree with this, vote 'no!'" And, so, expecting all of the boys to vote 'aye' and that I'd be "in good company and part of the group," I yelled out *in the loudest voice I could muster*, "*Aye*!" Well, I have to tell you, dear reader, I was the only one who voted that way! One of the boys said, "Well, I guess

Susie's still awake!" And the whole group laughed!
Again, I was clearly "out of step" with everyone else!

You know, dear reader, sometimes when we find that
we're clearly "out of step with it all" we learn valuable
lessons. In the Bible, for example, we read in Matthew
26:69-75, *"Now Peter was sitting outside in the court-
yard. And a maid came up to him, and said, 'You also
were with Jesus the Galilean.' But he denied it before
them all, saying, 'I do not know what you mean.' And
when he went out to the porch, another maid saw him,
and she said to the bystanders, 'This man was with Jesus
of Nazareth.' And again he denied it with an oath, 'I do
not know the man.' After a little while the bystanders
came up and said to Peter, 'Certainly you are also one of
them, for your accent betrays you.' Then he began to
invoke a curse on himself and to swear, 'I do not know the
man.' And immediately the cock crowed. And Peter
remembered the saying of Jesus, 'Before the cock crows,
you will deny me three times.' And he went out and wept
bitterly."*

In those verses we see that Peter wanted very much to be
just like all the other people. He did not want to be different from them. He didn't want to be "out of step" with
the others. He was looking for approval and acceptance
from the people around him. He said things that he hoped

would make him acceptable. Ultimately and unfortunately, the consequences of his actions were profound when he realized what he'd said. He hung his head in shame and wept. He had denied Jesus Christ!

In Matthew 10:32-33, we read, *"So every one who acknowledges me before men, I also will acknowledge before my Father who is in heaven; but whoever denies me before men, I also will deny before my Father who is in heaven."*

We might tend to be a little worried about poor Peter if our Bibles had not made mention of the fact that Peter became truly remorseful… *"he went out and wept bitterly."* He became repentant and undoubtedly begged for forgiveness.

As Christians, we often *need* to be "out of step" with the world around us, but when it comes to speaking about our Lord and Savior, Jesus Christ, we should *never* compromise our loyalty to or love for Him. It's too risky. What if something happened to us before we could repent and ask for forgiveness? The consequences would be horrible!

Prayer:
Oh, Lord, as I proceed along my pathway, today, help me to remember that it's o.k. to be *out of step with this world*

occasionally, but it's mandatory to *be in step with You...always!* Help me to remember that it's o.k. to be a *little different and maybe even a little odd* when compared to everyone else, if *I'm in step with You!*

Help me to know that you are always with me, leading me, guiding me, and protecting me...that in fact, You have promised in Deuteronomy 31:8 and Hebrews 13: 5, *"I will never fail you nor forsake you."* Help me to do likewise for You, O Lord! Help me to never deny You nor to make excuses for being one of Your followers. Help me, O Lord, to be steadfast in You and to grow in my Christian faith, day by day.

Amen

Devotional Reading #12

Changing Times

I think, dear reader, that if you thought about it for a little while you'd be able to recall some things in your past that likely would not happen in today's world…due to "changing times." If those things happened quite a while ago maybe you're *"living an analog life in a digital world."* You lived a life in simpler times and now, sometimes, you don't quite fit. Oh, you've tried to keep up with the changing times, but you've not been totally successful. You still remember, perhaps with fond memories, the way you once lived life. You're an "analog person living in a digital world" because of changing times.

For me, I can recall the early days of television. Television was just coming into being when I was a kid and people who owned TV's were few and far between. We couldn't afford such a luxury, but every Sunday my mom, dad (who was a Y.M.C.A. Physical Director) and I would go down to the Y.M.C.A. and, since no one was there, we had the place to ourselves. We'd get three straight-backed chairs, line them up in front of the TV set in the boy's lounge and we'd watch TV…just like rich people! We didn't even mind it when the picture disappeared due to poor reception. We'd watch the black and white "snow" until the picture returned...because, after all, we could *hear* the sound from the program we were watching!

One Sunday when the "snow" on the TV was especially bad and we'd gotten tired of watching it, the three of us (Mom, Dad, and I) went skinny dipping in the Y pool. Now, I have to tell you, *that* was a new and unusual experience! I wondered what all that strange "sea weed" was hanging in front of my face until I realized that it wasn't sea weed at all...it was my hair! I'd always worn a swim cap before and my hair had always been tucked up inside my cap.

Anyway...I've gotten off of the subject of the TV, sorry. Finally, after diligently saving our money and shopping around for a good deal, we got a TV of our own. Ahhh, sweet progress! There were *buses* running outside our house to take us downtown when we wanted to go, and we had a TV in our house! How progressive we were becoming!

Another evidence of "changing times" involved the barn-garage that was behind our house. It used to be a barn, complete with a hay loft and a trap door through which the hay was hoisted onto the second floor, but by the time I was born and growing up, the city had grown up around the property, and so it was no longer a barn, but a garage. Nevertheless, my girlfriend and I loved to pretend that it was "still the olden days" and so we played on the second floor, dubbed it our "bat and rat house" and enjoyed many adventures up there.

One day we decided that the barn was old, might catch on fire at any minute and so we needed a fire escape! We got a cord, tied loops in it for our feet, secured the end of it around a post and because my girlfriend was the bravest, decided that she should "test it out as our fire escape." Out the second story door she went!

Everything seemed to be A-ok until one of her feet couldn't find the next lower loop. Then her other foot slipped out of its loop and there she hung by her finger tips…from the second story of that old red barn!

The neighbor rushed out of her house and shouted, "What are you kids trying to do, get yourselves killed? Get her back inside that barn immediately or I'm going to tell your parents!"

Scared stiff, ashen white in her face, fingers aching from holding on, there she hung! The situation was critical! It was, after all, a long way to the ground below! We were on the second floor!

We worked together feverishly…tugging, pulling and exerting with every ounce of strength until finally, both of us wringing wet with sweat…we got her back inside the barn! We lay there gasping and trying to catch our breaths. Whew! That was too close for comfort! So much for the idea of a fire escape!

Both our barn-garage and our house were almost one hundred years old, so I suppose it was not unusual to have a bat present in either building. Now, dear reader, I hope you won't be offended at this story, but my dad liked to sleep at night in "the buff" and so one night I awakened to the sound of lots of shouting and screaming. It was the middle of the night and both parents were up, stomping around, yelling and making quite a commotion. It woke me up and when I entered their bedroom, there was Dad, standing on the bed, in the buff, swinging a golf club back and forth! A bat was flying around the room and Dad was determined to get it!

It was quite a scene and I have to tell you, dear reader, he hadn't played 54 holes of golf in one day in his younger years for nothing! Swinging that golf club for all he was worth, splat…he connected with that bat and sent it straight to bat heaven! And…if I live to be a hundred, I'll never forget that scene and the fate of that bat that night! Now, my girlfriend and I thought we had something worse than a bat in our upstairs barn-garage playhouse one day. We were up there playing when we noticed a gunny sack over on the floor in the corner. Sneaking up on it our imaginations took over and we thought maybe it contained a long forgotten treasure. Maybe we'd be rich! Maybe a robber had robbed a bank and hidden the loot there in the gunny sack! Maybe we'd found that loot and we'd be famous! Maybe we'd even get our pictures in the newspaper! Be that as it may, we had to approach this thing with caution! So, cautiously and together, we inched our way toward it and gently poked it with our feet!

Oh, my gosh…it moved! *It moved!*

We about jumped out of our skins! Scared stiff-less, we about knocked each other over…about climbed over each other…retreating! Imaginations hyped to the hilt, we figured some monster or worse yet, *a rat*, was in that sack!

Forget the treasure, forget the bank robber and the loot, we had something *alive* in that sack! Now we needed a stick, a weapon! We needed to *defend* ourselves! What if it, whatever *it* was, came out of that sack and attacked us? We couldn't take any chances, we might be *bitten* by that thing, whatever it was! Maybe it even had *rabies*! Maybe we'd be bitten by it and end up in the hospital or worse yet, *dead*!

So, weapon in hand and scared stiff, we began pushing that gunny sack down the flight of steps from the second floor to the first floor. Each step downward seemed like a victory as we whooped and hollered!

And, then, as the gunny sack neared the landing before the final four steps, a corner of the gunny sack opened and out walked...not a monster at all, not even a rat, but, of all things...a small, furry baby squirrel! Thus, the poor little thing was introduced to the world of "humans" and although I think he had a few bumps and bruises, lived to tell his momma about a "couple of strange kids" who had wild imaginations!

You know, dear reader, times really have changed. Today, we're living in "digital times" when everything is fast paced and computerized into numerical digits and coding. It's no longer an "analog world" when everything was measured and transmitted via a continuously variable quantity such as electrical voltage. Today, I think people are required to deal with far more issues that are far more complex and complicated.

But, what about you, dear reader? What has life been like for you? Are you able to look back on your lifetime and pick out a few events that were from a simpler time? Or can you recall a humorous event...or an event from your childhood that reflects how "times have changed?" Can you recall those events, perhaps, in light of the Lord's protection for you, (as in the example of the second story fire escape)?

Can you join with me and say the following prayer:

Prayer:
O, Lord, thank You for helping me recall some good memories from my younger life when, like the simple stories in this devotional reading, it was a simpler time...maybe because I was a child or because life was, indeed, just less complicated or complex.

Thank You, O Lord, that as I reflect back in time, I can see that You have been there...that, in fact, You've always been there...that You were there even before I gave my heart to You or asked You to be my personal Lord and Savior. I can see that there have been times when You've protected, guided, and directed me. I can see that, like a true potter, You have melded me, molded me, and then, used me in some unique or special way. I can also see that You've never "given up on me."

Oh, Lord, may I always start each day by asking You to be there. May I begin each new day by saying, come into my life, O Lord, and be my Lord and Savior! Come also,

Holy Spirit! Take my life this day and...protect me...guide me...direct me...and also, meld me...mold me...and use me! In Your precious name, Jesus.

Amen

Devotional Reading #13

From Here to There

In Biblical times, to go from "here to there" people had only about five choices of transportation. They could walk on foot, or they could ride on a donkey, a camel, a horse, or use a boat.

A man's wealth was measured in how many donkeys he owned. That's why, often in battle, it was important to not only win the battle, but to seize whatever donkeys the opponents had. In Numbers 31:54, the Israelites captured some 61,000 donkeys from the Midianites.

Donkeys were used for many purposes. Often called "beasts of burden," not only did people ride on them, but they were used to carry possessions and heavy loads. They were also used in wars for transporting, as well as in agricultural pursuits to till the soil.

Of course, for Christians, one of the most important references to "an ass" and "a donkey" was found in the Old Testament (Zechariah 9:9) where it was recorded *"...Lo, your king comes to you; triumphant and victorious is he, humble and riding on an ass, on a colt, the foal of an ass,"* and then that verse was fulfilled in the New

Testament (Matthew 21:1-9) where it was recorded that Jesus' disciples went into the village to secure the colt of an ass for Jesus to ride upon as he entered Jerusalem on what came to be known as His triumphal entry on Palm Sunday.

Clearly, donkeys were important in the lives of the Israelites for transportation and many other uses.

Camels were also important. There were two kinds of camels, and they differed greatly in what they were used for and the speed at which they could travel. The two-humped camels could carry up to 400 pounds, but could only travel about 30 miles a day. The single humped camels had longer legs, would carry lighter weighted burdens, and could travel about 150 miles in a day. They were used for carrying messages and people from place to place.

Camels were used for not only transporting goods and people, but for pulling chariots and aiding the cavalry in times of battle.

Camel hair was used for making cloth, while the hides were used for making clothing. In Matthew 3:4 and Mark 1:6, we read about John the Baptist, *"Now John wore a garment of camel's hair, and a leather girdle around his waist..."*

The people of Israel didn't eat camel meat, as it was considered "unclean," but they did drink the camel's milk!

One of the best-known references to a camel in the New Testament was found in Matthew 19:24, which reads, *"Again I tell you, it is easier for a camel to go through the eye of a needle than for a rich man to enter the kingdom of God."* That verse can be understood in the context of Biblical times. In those days when the gates to the city were closed for the night and someone with a camel wanted to enter the city it was necessary to use one of the smaller gates. To enter through the smaller gate the camel had to be unloaded of its burdens and then lowered to its knees. Then, little by little, the camel was coaxed through the entrance while still on its knees. Thus, the analogy with the gate opening, *"it is easier for a camel to go through the eye of a needle than for a rich man to enter the kingdom of God."*

Horses were also important in Biblical times. In the Old Testament, in 1 Kings 10:28, it reads, *"And Solomon's import of horses was from Egypt and Kue, and the king's traders received them from Kue at a price."* (Kue was believed to be Cilicia, in Southeast Asia Minor, bordered on the north and west by the Taurus Mountains and on the south by the Mediterranean Sea). It was recorded in 1 Kings 10:26 that Solomon had 12,000 horses. *"And*

Solomon gathered together chariots and horsemen; he had fourteen hundred chariots and twelve thousand horsemen, whom he stationed in the chariot cities and with the king in Jerusalem."

In Esther 3:13, it was recorded that *"Letters were sent by couriers to all the king's provinces..."* A "pony express" of that day used horses and riders stationed a day's ride apart on all major roads, giving the country an effective means of communication.

Horses not only helped carry messages throughout the country, but they were used in agriculture, in royal processions when officers rode on them, plus in the battles of war.

Of course, horses were also symbolic of different things. In the Old Testament, in Zechariah 1: 8, we read, *"I saw in the night, and behold, a man riding upon a red horse! He was standing among the myrtle trees in the glen; and behind him were red, sorrel, and white horses."* The *red horse* symbolized bloodshed and war, maybe even internal revolution. In Zechariah 5:2, we read, *"The first chariot had red horses, the second black horses, the third white horses, and the fourth chariot dappled gray horses."* The *black horse* symbolized famine. The *dappled gray or pale horse* symbolized death and the *white horse* symbolized conquest. Some of those horses were also referred to in the New Testament, especially in Revelation 6:8 and 19:11.

The other form of transportation, namely, boats, is discussed in devotional reading #19.

Today, while we have planes, trains, buses, trucks, and other means of transportation, our main method of getting *from here to there* is the car. Do you remember learning to drive a car? Do you remember the excitement of sitting behind the wheel for the first time? Who taught you what to do? Was it a driving school instructor, a parent, or maybe a friend? What experiences did you have during those days of learning to drive? Can you remember?

For me, when I was about fifteen years old or so mom and dad took me out for driving lessons. In those days a teenager didn't have the option to enroll in a driving school, so it was usually mom and dad who did the educational training in how to drive a car. I remember we had a 1953 gray and white Pontiac and once in a while when we'd go out for a Sunday afternoon drive in the country they'd let me drive the car. Like any teenage kid, I looked forward to getting my driver's license and someday owning my own car. One day after I'd been driving for considerable miles I was tired with the stress and strain of it all and so I pulled over to let dad take over the driving. We switched seats and after driving for just a short distance, dad said, "What's wrong with the steering on this car? Something's wrong here. It feels like we've got a flat tire!"

Well, sure enough! When he stopped the car and looked, lo and behold, I'd been driving along for goodness knows how long...on a flat tire! No wonder I was tired with the stress and strain of it all! Fighting that wheel to keep the car going straight ahead had worn me out!

Needless to say, when I signed up to take the road test for a driver's license, I was as nervous as a cat on a hot tin roof. I wasn't used to having a stranger, and an officer, to boot, sitting in the front seat with me as I drove. He sat there in his starched white shirt with his clipboard, periodically making notes and checking off things. It bummed me out! I couldn't seem to do anything right. Do you know that it took me *four* tries before I passed that road test? I was beginning to think I was destined to do a *lot* of walking in my life!

After we moved to St. Paul, Dad always liked to take our car back to Winona, Minnesota, where he'd purchased it to get it serviced. So, periodically, he'd make an appointment for car maintenance of some kind or another and we'd drive the hundred and twenty-some miles to Winona. The car dealer was located near the downtown area so to "pass the time away," maybe two to three hours or so, Mom, Dad, and I would walk over to the Winona Hotel and sit in their lobby. Now, the Winona Hotel was *the* best hotel in the city! Nothing shabby about that hotel!

There we sat in the lobby of that hotel, the three of us! Dad would read one of the magazines and then I'd see the inevitable begin to happen. Sitting in one of the hotel's big cushy, comfy chairs while still holding the magazine with one hand, I'd see Dad's other hand start to move down along the inside of the chair. He was up to his favorite "trick" again…checking out the chair for money that had fallen out of someone else's pocket!

As a kid, I noticed this routine, and so it wasn't long before I was doing it too. On the drive down to Winona we'd speculate on who'd find the most money! It was something to look forward to and we did! First one of dad's hands would go down along the inside of the chair he was sitting in, and then the other hand would go down along the other side of the chair! Nevertheless, the *real* challenge was checking out the *back inside* of the chair! Now that took some real ingenuity, as we didn't want to appear obvious about what we were doing!

101

Finally, all was completed and the chair was checked to satisfaction. Then, we'd sit back and rest awhile so as to not make anyone suspicious of what we were up to!

Gradually then, we'd move on to another chair and go through the whole process all over again. Well, I have to tell you…Dad and I made our way around every chair in that hotel lobby! And, meanwhile, my mother sat idly by and just shook her head, pretending that she didn't know us!

Nevertheless, Dad and I loved this game…and if we were successful (and we usually were) we had some extra money with which to purchase an ice cream sundae after the car was finished being serviced.

Later on in life when I married my husband, John, he had a wonderful car that I absolutely loved. It was a 1967 Ford Galaxy. It was a sleek looking metallic blue, four-door hardtop that my husband affectionately named "Betsy." Betsy was a superb car, one I always loved to ride in! Nevertheless, the first time John dated me and I was riding in the front seat, he slammed on the brakes; I slid right off that front seat and got acquainted with the floor!

Unfortunately, Betsy met up a few too many times with the salty winter roads of Minnesota and her frame rusted out. One day while we were driving, John hit a good sized pot hole in the road and the frame broke! Nevertheless, the fixit man that John was, he thought maybe it could be fixed if he could just get Betsy home where he could take a good look at her and ascertain how bad the damage was; until then, there was hope she could be fixed.

So, John tied a rope to the frame of that car and with the passenger side door ajar, I held up the bottom of that car while John drove us home! When we got Betsy home we almost took the side of the garage off before we realized that the back wheels were about a foot off to the side of the front wheels. The car had run...well...sideways! We couldn't even get the car into the garage! It was a sad day, indeed, when the tow truck came and towed Betsy away to the junk yard! We felt like we'd lost a dearly departed loved one!

Because so much of life today, in 21st Century America, depends on the use of a car...this devotional reading will end with a prayer for your driving or riding in a car, dear reader.

Prayer:
O Lord, I ask for protection today as I am "out and about." I ask that as I drive my car or ride in a car (or some other means of transportation), that You are with

me…protecting me. Help me to be alert to the presence of other people near me and to speculate on what their intentions might be. Help me to, in a sense, drive (or ride in) the other vehicles around me as well as my own. Help me to be observant! Help me to avoid confrontations with people who might not be paying attention to what they're doing, people who appear stressed out or angry. Help me to be courteous and patient with other people. Help me to be kind and considerate of other people. Help me to keep my mind on what I'm doing and where I'm going.

Please send my guardian angel to be ever present with me…protecting me from any harm that might threaten to overtake me. Watch over me, O Lord, and bring me safely to my destinations and to end my day successfully. I ask this in Your Holy and Precious Name, Jesus.

Amen

Devotional Reading #14

Talents

Have you ever been in a school talent show, dear reader? Have you ever performed some sort of talent act in front of an audience? Have you ever played the piano, sang a song, or done something else...in front of an audience?

I think school talent shows are always interesting. There are talented students...some of which play musical instruments, twirl a baton, do acrobatics, read a poem or any number of things. As a junior high school student, I was in the school talent show performing an unusual talent...Indian Club twirling. In the years prior to the school talent show Dad had taught the boys at the Y (and me, his daughter) a most unique "Indian Club Drill." Dad often said that Indian Club Drills had, at one time, been part of the early Olympics and that men had competed for Olympic medals by performing the complexities of the drills.

Basically, Indian Clubs were like small bowling pins and the Indian Club Drills involved holding onto the small knob at the end of a club, one in each hand, and going through a series of circles, big and small around the upper part of the body.

Every two years my dad involved the Y boys in a Gym Show at which the public paid admission. It was a good show, well worth the small admission price required! The shows gave the boys something to shoot for, something to work toward and they performed a variety of activities…marching pyramids, ladder pyramids, apparatus work (such as the vault, horse, parallel bars, etc.), and since Mom taught the Y "girls classes" there were soft shoe routines, dance numbers, rhythmic ball numbers, etc. One weekend every two years, with three performances, those Gym Shows were looked forward to by many people!

Thus, when it was announced at my junior high school that there would be a talent show, two boy classmates and I decided to perform the Indian Club Drill together.

We thought we'd really impress the audience and do the drill with fire on the end of the clubs. We'd done that before at the Y, so it was not new for us. There were two talent show performances at school and the first performance went off like clockwork. We were a big hit! We were the last act and liked to think that "they'd saved the best 'til the last!"

But then, in between the two shows we were busy…we had to take the burned wads of cotton off the ends of the clubs, wad up new balls of cotton and nail them to the ends of the clubs for the next show. That part of the act we'd never done before and, being nervous and in too big of a hurry, we wadded up too much cotton and didn't nail it to the clubs securely enough. We also got too much Mineral Spirit fluid on the cotton wads and didn't squeeze them out nearly enough. But, we didn't know any of that until we began our act during the second show.

Suddenly, a tuft of cotton flew off the end of a club and alighted in the hair of one of the boys. He had to interrupt his drill to "put out the fire in his hair." He stood there beating on his head to put it out! Then, another tuft of cotton flew off and landed on the floor. I had to interrupt my drill to stomp out that small fire on the floor. Then, another tuft of cotton flew off and landed on the stage curtain. It started burning and within seconds the janitor rushed up on stage with a broom and began beating the curtain.

By that time the entire audience of kids was on their feet! No one was left sitting! They didn't know what to think! They didn't know whether that was part of the act or not. Then, one of the kids yelled, "Hey, the school's on fire…we won't have to go to school tomorrow!"

Well, I have to tell you, years later…many years later…when I happened to be at the Y working out in the exercise room who should be there also, but the Principal from that junior high school! When I greeted him, he looked at me for a minute and then he said, "Didn't you go to the junior high school where I was the Principal?" I said, "Yes." And then he asked, "Do you remember that talent show where that one act caught the curtains on fire and almost burned down the school?"

Well, I have to tell you, dear reader, I made a rather hasty retreat from the room, mumbling as I went that "my exercise time was up and that I had to leave!" I don't know if, after all those years, he just got lucky in saying what he did to me because I was about the right age, or if I did look familiar to him as having caused that trouble, but I didn't stick around long enough to find out!

In the book of Matthew, chapter 25, verses 14-30, we see the word "talent" but it doesn't refer to a "natural mental, creative, or artistic ability" as in the case of a school "talent," show. Instead, in the Bible, a "talent" refers to an amount of money. It is believed that a talent in Biblical days was probably worth about a thousand dollars.

In Matthew 25:14-30, a man called his servants to him and since he was going on a journey, he wanted to entrust his property to them while he was gone. To one servant he gave five talents ($5,000), to another two talents

($2,000) and to another servant he gave one talent ($1,000). He gave each servant money according to his abilities. Then, the man went on his journey.

In verses 16-18, we read, *"He who had received the five talents went at once and traded with them, and he made five talents more. So also, he who had the two talents made two talents more. But he who had received the one talent went and dug in the ground and hid his master's money."*

Going on in verses 19-30, we read, *"Now after a long time the master of those servants came and settled accounts with them. And he who had received the five talents came forward, bringing five talents more, saying 'Master, you delivered to me five talents; here, I have made five talents more.' His master said to him, 'Well done, good and faithful servant; you have been faithful over much; enter into the joy of your master.' And he also who had the two talents came forward, saying, 'Master, you delivered to me two talents; here I have made two talents more.' His master said to him, 'Well done, good and faithful servant; you have been faithful over a little, I will set you over much; enter into the joy of your master.' He also who had received the one talent came forward, saying, 'Master, I knew you to be a hard man, reaping where you did not sow, and gathering where you did not win-*

now; so I was afraid and I went and hid your talent in the ground. Here you have what is yours.' But his master answered him, 'You wicked and slothful servant! You knew that I reap where I have not sowed, and gather where I have not winnowed? Then you ought to have invested my money with the bankers, and at my coming I should have received what was my own with interest. So take the talent from him, and give it to him who has the ten talents. For to every one who has will more be given, and he will have abundance; but from him who has not, even what he has will be taken away. And cast the worthless servant into the outer darkness; there men will weep and gnash their teeth.'"

In this devotional reading, therefore, we have two types of "talents." One "talent" refers to a person's natural, mental, creative, or artistic ability and the other use of the word refers to money, probably about a thousand dollars in today's monetary equivalent.

The lesson we might learn is that we must always use our "talents" wisely.

Prayer:
Oh, Heavenly Father, help me to use my natural talents, be they God-given mental, creative, or artistic talents to their fullest, because they have been given to me as gifts

from You. As it says in 1 Corinthians 7:7, *"...each has his own special gift from God, one of one kind and one of another."* If I have been taught something by someone and it has become my talent, help me to use that talent wisely and be a credit to God and my teacher. And finally, O Lord, in the use of my money, as reflected in the Biblical use of the word "talent," help me to be wise in saving, investing, tithing or spending my money as befitting a good Christian.

Amen

Spectacular Vistas

Have you ever climbed a mountain, dear reader, or have you ever scaled a rocky ledge? Or perhaps, when you were younger, you scampered up a hill and reached the top before your parents did? Can you remember looking out at the valley below and feeling like you were on top of the world, amazed at the spectacular vista before you? Can you remember how vast the scene was and how small the things beneath you were? If so, come along with me now while I tell you about climbing one of the Rocky Mountain peaks in Colorado.

During the summers when I was going to college I worked at the National Y.M.C.A. Association Camp near Estes Park, Colorado. Being a "Y brat" (affectionately called that since I was the daughter of a Y.M.C.A. Physical Director), I was fortunate enough to be selected to join the 500 or so college students who'd been carefully screened and selected to work there for the summer months, June until September.

On the days when employees weren't working around the camp, they were often mountain climbing. I was no exception, as the peaks in the Rocky Mountain National

Park were abundant and every one climbed was considered an accomplishment. The ultimate goal for most employees was to climb the highest peak, Longs Peak, which reached a height of 14,255 feet. To do that, however, it was necessary to have completed the prerequisites of first climbing a twelve and then a thirteen thousand foot mountain.

Now, I'd always had a little fear of heights, but little did I know how much that fear would be put to the test when I climbed Longs. The trek began at midnight at the base of the mountain using flashlights to see our way. Does that strike you as odd? Nevertheless, that's the way it's done, because in Colorado, there are often noon-hour or early-afternoon electrical storms that come up, and so hikers and climbers must be off the mountain summit by then or it could be very dangerous. With no trees there, since it's above timberline, the people are the tallest objects up there and lightning strikes are no fun...especially when *you* are the object of them!

The hike upwards progressed until the "cable section" was reached. At that point, the side of the mountain was almost vertical, straight up and down. There was a cable attached to the side of the mountain and for a distance of maybe seventy-five feet (I don't remember exactly) climbers had to grasp the cable in both hands, plant their feet against the mountainside and "walk" up that mountain! Let me tell you, for a person battling a fear of height, that challenge was almost more than I could handle! Nevertheless, determined to succeed, I grasped that cable for all I was worth and pulled myself along it, progressing upwards inch by inch! By the time I reached the end of it, at the top, my legs felt like "wobbly jello," and I was shaking like a leaf!

One by one, the entire climbing party made it to the top of that cable! But, as I sat there regaining the strength in my body, I wondered how on earth I was ever going to go *down* that cable!

The summit was reached shortly thereafter and with great pride we all signed the "summit log" that's often atop Rocky Mountain peaks. Staying just long enough to snap a few photos of that spectacular vista and throw a few snowballs, we soon began our journey downwards.

We hadn't descended very far before we met some other climbers coming to the summit. One of those climbers we stopped to talk with because he wasn't your average mountain climber! He was crippled! His legs were small and underdeveloped and he used arm crutches to help himself navigate! Since we weren't far from the summit when we met that brave soul, we knew that, yes, he would make it to the summit! Amazing courage, that fellow!

I think seeing him made it easier for me to tackle that cable going downwards. It wasn't as hard as I had thought it would be! And, so, my mountain climbing experience of Longs Peak ended...from there on down it was "a piece of cake!" I'd done it! All 14,255 feet of it!

Dear reader, life has many "mountain-peak challenges!" There are many things that come along in our lives that cause us to wonder if we can conquer them. Sometimes it's a schooling challenge or a job challenge, maybe it's a sickness challenge, or maybe it's a relationship challenge with a family member or a friend. "Mountain peak challenges" can take many forms! Nevertheless, whatever the challenges that confront you, the Lord is there to help you with them. If you call upon him, He will come to your aid.

Prayer:
Oh, Lord, I ask that You be with me to face the challenges of this day. Whether they be small in nature or mountain peak in scope, help me to think of and keep my eyes on You, always "looking upward." Help me know what You want me to do in the challenges set before me this day. Help me to hear Your voice and Your promptings that I

might choose the right course of action. Help me to remember, in the midst of my concerns, that there is no challenge, no problem, that You can't help me with and that You will be there with me…by my side…through it all.

Please come into my life anew and afresh right now, O Lord. I ask You to come! And, please, Lord, take my hand and lead me through whatever challenges the hours of this day bring me.

And then I ask, O Lord, that later, perhaps at the day's end, that You help me to be able to look back and to recall the ways, small or great, in which Your presence was obvious…ways in which You were definitely there with me and/or for me!

I ask these things in Your precious name, Lord Jesus.

Amen

Devotional Reading #16

Serving

In Luke 10:38-42, it says: *"Now as they went on their way, he (Jesus) entered a village; and a woman named Martha received him into her house. And she had a sister called Mary, who sat at the Lord's feet and listened to his teaching. But Martha was distracted with much serving; and she went to him and said, 'Lord, do you not care that my sister has left me to serve alone? Tell her then to help me.' But the Lord answered her, 'Martha, Martha, you are anxious and troubled about many things; one thing is needful. Mary has chosen the good portion, which shall not be taken away from her.'"*

These verses are often quoted when it's desirable to point out that Mary chose to be with her Lord over and above anything else while Martha thought it important that she serve Him and the other guests…that she wait on them and tend to their needs. While Mary's choice is often upheld as the better of the two women's choices because the times of being with the Lord were few in number (Mary seized the opportunity to be with Him and learn from Him…an opportunity that she recognized as priceless!) nevertheless, we see in Martha, her sister, someone who had a "servant's heart." Some people are born with that God-given attribute and they are happiest when they can "serve or wait on" someone else. We can look at the lives of many people (i.e., Mother Theresa of Calcutta, caregivers of sick and infirmed, perhaps handicapped, elderly or dying people, nurses, Red Cross volunteers, disaster workers, etc.) who have responded to the needs of those around them. Those people have "servant's hearts" and they are to be admired and thanked for their helpfulness and kindnesses.

Thus, in those Bible verses, we can learn two things: (1) from Mary we can learn that it's best to put the Lord first in our lives, but (2) from Martha we can learn that an attribute of our love for Him exhibits itself when we can serve or help someone else.

Now, in my own life, while I earnestly try to keep the Lord "on the throne of my life," I do, nevertheless, have a servant's heart. I love doing things for other people. It just comes naturally for me. I try to remember other people's likes and dislikes and to respond accordingly. I love making little gifts for people. I love helping them in whatever ways I can. I don't strive to do those things, they're just natural for me. God put a servant's heart within me!

Nevertheless, I have to tell you, dear reader, in the job of "waitress" I was not so good! Oh, I wanted to wait on those customers and do a good job, but I don't know, maybe I tried too hard to please them! Well, whatever the reason, perhaps you'll be amused as you read about my efforts.

For my summer job, I was chosen to be a waitress in "The Pine Room," an exclusive and very nice guest's dining room. Wearing my little starched white apron, my boss, big Bertha, called me "Blondie," because in those days I loved being a bleached blonde every summer. Every young twenty-something young-thing in those days knew that "blondes have more fun" and I was ready for it!

It turned out, however, that I wasn't very good at the art of being a waitress. One evening I had a large party of people to take the orders for and the specialty of the evening was "lamb chops." One order consisted of three lamb chops. So, being the inexperienced young waitress that I was and wanting to help the cook in the kitchen understand the order better, I decided to write on my order ticket...three lamb chops and what that person wanted to go with it, potatoes, vegetable, etc. Then, for the next person, I did the same thing...three lamb chops and what that person wanted to go with them. That I did for each of the people who ordered lamb chops...and submitted the order to the cook in the kitchen.

Now, time went by and the order wasn't ready. The guests started to get antsy! They threatened to leave if their orders didn't arrive soon. So, in all haste, I scurried into the kitchen to check on their order.

I approached the big Texan cook, Larry, who, with blood shot eyes and a sweat stained T shirt, stood in front of that huge hot stove, when I hollered, "Larry, what's wrong? Where's my order? The people are getting antsy and are about to leave. Where's that order of mine?"

He looked at me with his blood shot eyes as he mopped his brow. And then, arm extended and with a circular motion, he gestured to the partially filled trays with dishes awaiting lamb chops. They were everywhere! He'd thought I meant three *orders* of lamb chops every time I'd written "three lamb chops!" That made for 36 orders of lamb chops!

Oh, man! I couldn't believe it! And, I have to tell you, it was a good thing that the boss had the night off because everyone in the whole kitchen ate free lamb chops that night! There were about 12 orders too many! I think the camp must have had an excess of lamb chops supplied to them that summer, because we employees were often served lamb chops for our evening meal. I don't know if it was that waitressing blunder with them or not, but from that night onwards I couldn't stand lamb chops! I'd find out that lamb chops were on the menu for the employees' meal that night and I either went hungry or hustled on down to the camp snack bar and bought myself a hamburger!

Another time when I was waitressing there I was carrying a big tray of desserts...slices of ice cream rolls with nut meats around the outsides, and I accidentally brushed the top of a lady's head with the tray. Unbeknownst to me, there were some nut meats stuck on the under side of the tray and when I brushed the top of her head a whole pile was deposited right smack in the middle of the part on the top of her head! Now what do you do...stand there and pick them off, or ignore them like you don't see them? Well, I have to tell you, I did the latter. But, I've always wondered what she thought when she got home, combed her hair, and saw all of those nut meats fall out!

Back home in Minnesota, one summer I got a job as a waitress in a very exclusive country club. (I told them I had lots of waitressing experience, can you imagine that?) There too, however, it seemed as though waitressing jobs weren't my forte! I'd taken the drink orders and went about distributing them to the guests when a guest turned around, accidentally bumping my arm! Swoosh! A whole glass of iced tea went down a guy's back! Man, you never saw a guy move so fast!

I felt just awful, but the damage had been done! And, then, to make it worse, when I offered to go to the guy's house and get him a clean shirt, (as if I could do that in the first place, without a key!) the guy said, "That was my last clean shirt!" Oh, no…

Thus, it was that I decided that maybe future jobs ought to involve doing something other than waitressing!

Prayer:
Oh Lord, today as I go about my activities, help me to remember that You need to be "on the throne of my life"…You need to be *the* most important thing in my life. Help me to *think* thoughts that are pleasing to You. Help me to *do* things that are pleasing to You. Help me to picture You there, *with me*, in whatever I think or do. Help me to remember Your words in Luke from today's reading, when You spoke indicating that Mary had chosen the good portion…the good portion which is You, O Lord, and that that portion shall not be taken from her. But help me, also, to remember Martha, who had a servant's heart. Help me to serve others in whatever way that I can today, to show forth love for other people. And in so doing, to exemplify Your love for us, O Lord. You loved us so much that You were willing to die for us that we might be made acceptable to God, the Father. When You died upon the cross for our sins, O Lord, You exemplified the ulti-

mate in having a "servant's heart!" You came that we might have life and have it abundantly! We thank You and we praise You! In Jesus' Name,

Amen

Wind

One winter break from college I took the Rock Island Line train to Denver where I caught a bus to Estes Park. There, the Y.M.C.A. van picked me up and took me to Camp where I planned to work for two weeks. The Camp hosted various families and groups of people during the winter, and since I'd been a summer employee, it was natural that I resumed my job as waitress in the Pine Room Dining Hall. I was delighted to be there, especially since the night before my arrival a beautiful blanket of snow had fallen, giving the Camp a picture postcard look!

Most staff members during the winter months were "year-round employees," so the most convenient place for me to stay was in the Camp Infirmary. It had to be heated, anyway, in the event that someone got sick or there was an emergency. Thus, with not much thought about it, I unpacked.

The previous summer when I'd been out there there'd been a mountain climbing accident and one of the employees had been killed. It had been, of course, a tragic event that had grieved the whole camp.

In the Infirmary, all alone that first night, I began remembering that tragedy when I saw the stained gurney used to bring him down the mountainside. It was propped up against the Infirmary wall and seeing it didn't help my imagination much. Then, outside, as the nighttime dragged on, the wind got stronger and stronger as it whistled through the pine trees, causing swaying branches to scrape against the roof. Have you ever noticed how foreboding and eerie the wind sounds when you're alone in a strange place at night? Well, dear reader, I have to tell you, my imagination went into overdrive when the furnace switched on and it sounded like a door opening! I can tell you, I slept with the lights on...the whole two weeks I was there!

In this devotional reading now let's turn to the Holy Bible to see what it has to say about the subject of "wind."

In Genesis 8:1-5, we read, *"But God remembered Noah and all the beasts and all the cattle that were with him in the ark. And God made a wind blow over the earth, and the waters subsided; the fountains of the deep and the windows of the heavens were closed, the rain from the heavens was restrained, and the waters receded from the earth continually. At the end of a hundred and fifty days the waters had abated; and in the seventh month, and on the seventeenth day of the month, the ark came to rest upon the mountains of Ararat. And the waters continued to abate until the tenth month, on the first day of the month, the tops of the mountains were seen. "*

In Greek and Hebrew the word "wind" can refer to "breath" or "spirit," and so when God "made a wind to blow over the earth" it might be likened to God breathing over the earth. He breathed on the earth "and the waters subsided."

Of course, we know that wind comes from different directions when it blows across the earth. In the Bible, the "east wind" is mentioned the most and is generally indicative of a storm or something destructive. The "north wind" is refreshing and may bring rain. The "south wind" is a gentle, soothing wind that helps crops grow, while the "west wind" blows away stagnant air.

In Exodus 10:13-19 it says, *"So Moses stretched forth his rod over the land of Egypt, and **the Lord brought an east wind** (emphasis added) upon the land all that day and all that night; and when it was morning the east wind had **brought the locusts** (emphasis added). And the locusts came up over all the land of Egypt, and settled over the whole country of Egypt, such a dense swarm of locusts as had never been before, nor ever shall be again. For they covered the face of the whole land, so that the land was darkened, and they ate all the plants in the land and all* *the fruit of the trees which the hail had left; not a green thing remained, neither tree nor plant of the field, through all the land of Egypt. Then Pharaoh called Moses and Aaron in haste, and said, 'I have sinned against the Lord your God, and against you. Now therefore, forgive my sin, I pray you, only this once, and entreat the Lord your God only to remove this death from me.' So he went out from Pharaoh, and entreated the Lord. **And the Lord turned a very strong west wind** (emphasis added), which lifted the locusts and drove them into the Red Sea; not a single locust was left in all the country of Egypt."* (You can continue reading this story by referring to Exodus 10:20, onwards).

So, in those verses we see the effects of both the east and west winds in the lives of the Israelites and Egyptians. One wind brought the locusts to the area and the other wind carried the locusts away.

Of course, figuratively, when mentioned in Scriptures, the word "wind" can also refer to the *judgments of God* (Jeremiah 22:22, Hosea 13:15, and Matthew 7:25), *of heresy* (Ephesians 4:14) or *the Holy Spirit* (1 Kings 19: 11, Ezekiel 37:9-10, 14, or in John 3:8, and Acts 2:2).

It's the latter that I'd like to conclude this devotional reading with…a short discussion that the Holy Spirit is often present as a "wind," and it's synonymous with "breath" of God.

In Ezekiel 36 and 37, the account is given of the Israelites returning to the "Valley of Dry Bones." The Lord God said, in Ezekiel 36:24, *"For I will take you from the nations, and gather you from all the countries, and bring you into your own land."* And then, in Ezekiel 37:3, the question was asked, *"...can these bones live?"* Verse 14 says, *"I will put my Spirit within you, and you shall live, and I will place you in your own land; then you shall know that I, the Lord, have spoken, and I have done it, says the Lord."*

In those verses God breathed (synonymous with the word "wind"...as "a wind came into them from God") on the people and they came alive! The bones in the Valley of Dry Bones began to rattle and come together as God breathed life into the people.

Then, in the New Testament, in Acts 2:2, we read, *"When the day of Pentecost had come, they were all together in one place. And suddenly a sound came from heaven like the rush of a mighty wind, and it filled all the house where they were sitting. And there appeared to them tongues as of fire, distributed and resting on each one of them. And they were all filled with the Holy Spirit and began to speak in other tongues, as the Spirit gave them utterance."*

Thus, in those verses it's seen that the arrival of the Holy Spirit was accompanied by the sound of a mighty rushing wind! And, thus, full of power, the Holy Spirit appeared as "tongues of fire" resting on the people!

With the touch of the Holy Spirit the people began to manifest unusual and supernatural powers. Acts 2:6, says, "And at this sound (*the mighty rushing wind,* clarification added) the multitude came together, and they were bewildered, because each one heard them speaking in his own language."

A mighty rushing wind accompanied, was part of, and ushered in the Holy Spirit. Of course, the Holy Spirit is worthy of a study in itself, but this reading will conclude by citing what that mighty rushing wind brought with it when it accompanied, was part of, and ushered in the Holy Spirit…the gifts and the fruits of the Holy Spirit, things that we should all seek for ourselves.

In Galatians 5:22-23, the fruits of the Spirit are listed and they are: love, joy, peace, patience, kindness, goodness, faithfulness, gentleness, and self-control. In 1 Corinthians 12:4-10, the gifts of the Holy Spirit are listed and they are: wisdom, knowledge, faith, healing, working of miracles, prophecy, discernment, tongues, and the interpretation of tongues.

Prayer:
Oh, Heavenly Father, forgive me for my sins, cleanse me from all unrighteousness and let the winds of Your Holy Spirit fall on me and fill me with the fruits and gifts that You desire me to have. Fill me to overflowing, Lord, that I may be about the work of Your kingdom here on earth!

Amen

Trees

Have you ever looked at the trees that grow along the timberline in mountains? Have you noticed how they're shaped and how their shapes show a hard fought battle for survival? Many trees are gnarled and twisted with greenery only appearing on one side of the tree, the side away from prevailing winds and raging storms. Some of the trees at timberline are decades old, yet they're stunted in growth and are little larger than bushes. Nevertheless, all are uniquely fascinating, well worth the time spent in really looking at them and even studying them.

One winter when I was in Colorado I decided to try mountain skiing. So, after renting equipment, I spotted a chair lift and hurriedly sat down on the first chair that came along. The air was crisp and fresh, the snow conditions excellent, and I was excited to fulfill my dream of skiing in the mountains! Nevertheless, as I sat there on the chair lift I spotted a big sign I'd missed in my haste to get on the empty chair lift. The sign showed all of the downhill runs at the ski area and for the first time since I'd gotten there, I realized how big the ski area was! Oh, well, the day was before me, and I was looking forward to the challenges ahead!

Skiers went whizzing down the mountainside beneath me and, as I ascended, the panoramic view around me was spectacular! It was a winter wonderland! How great was God to have created such beauty and magnificence! How wonderful to be a part of it on that ski lift!

Soon, however, I began to notice that it was getting colder...a *lot* colder! I started to shiver! There were fewer skiers, less trees and still the chair lift continued to climb. The lift passed timberline and *still* it continued upwards! Then it dawned on me, I should've checked that big map of the area at the bottom of the chairlift before I got on the lift! Clearly, not for beginners or novices, I was on the chairlift for the experts!

After a ride that seemed to last forever, cold and shivering, I looked upwards and saw the mountain's summit and the end of the chairlift!

Thank goodness! But, with about one hundred and fifty feet to go to the end of the lift, there, tacked onto a high pole, was a huge mirror with a sign over it that said, "Check for frostbite!" "Wow!" I thought, "How frightening! I'm not even sure what frostbite looks like. I wouldn't know if I had it or not."

Nevertheless, I got off the chairlift all right, but what bummed me out was a lady lying on the snow sobbing hysterically, and crying, "How am I ever going to get down from this mountainside? I don't know how to ski."

Well, dear reader, that sounded familiar to me, as I was wondering the same thing about myself. But, I figured that I'd gotten myself into that predicament and I had to get myself out! So, dear reader, I "side stepped" most of the way down that vertical mountainside. It was so steep there was no other way to do it!

As I did so, expert skiers whizzed by me shouting, "Are you ok? Do you need help?" And, I'd yell back, "I'm fine and no, I don't need help!"

Well, soon trees came into view and I was back within timberline! Ahhhhh, sweet trees and lower altitudes!

Do you know, dear reader, that within the Holy Bible there are over 300 references to trees and wood, plus there are over 25 different kinds of trees that have been identified as having grown within the Holy Lands?

In the days of the Old Testament, the lands of Canaan (which included the coastland between Egypt and Asia Minor) and Syria, except for the tops of mountains, were covered with forests.

You could, quite literally, make a study of the Bible based on a study of trees and the types of wood mentioned. Such a study would give you, I think, a different insight into the lives and times of people in both the Old and New Testaments. Beginning in Genesis 2:16-17, where the Lord God said to Adam in the Garden of Eden, "You may freely eat of every tree of the garden; but of the *tree of knowledge* (emphasis added) of good and evil you shall not eat, for in the day that you eat of it you shall die," right on through the whole Bible until Revelation 2:1-7, where, warning the city of Ephesus that their love of God had grown cold and if they didn't repent he'd be angry, it's said, "He who has an ear, let him hear what the Spirit says to the churches. To him who conquers I will grant to eat of the *tree of life* (emphasis added), which is in the paradise of God."

Taken alphabetically and mentioning only eleven different kinds of trees found in the Bible, we can learn several things in this devotional reading.

The *acacia tree,* in Exodus 27:1, was used to build the altar on which Israelites made sacrifices to their God. It says, *"You shall make the altar of acacia wood, five cubits long and five cubits broad; the altar shall be square, and its height shall be three cubits."* The altar measured about eight feet square and five feet in height.

Acacia wood was a hard, close-grained wood, not easily damaged by water, fire or heat from the continuous flames that burned in the center of the altar over-laid with a piece of bronze and where sacrifices were burned. Acacia wood was also used to build the tabernacle, the Ark of the Covenant, and other sacred objects.

In 2 Chronicles 9:10-11, Solomon used *algum wood* in the construction of the temple. "And the king made of the algum wood steps for the house of the Lord and for the king's house, lyres also and harps for the singers; there never was seen the like of them before in the land of Judah." Algum wood was a sweet-scented wood of strength, beauty and long life that took a high polish.

The *almond tree* was the first to bloom in Spring in the Judean Desert. In Genesis 30:37, Aaron used rods fashioned out of poplar and almond branches to keep his flocks of sheep at the watering troughs. In Exodus 25: 33-36, it mentioned that the bowls of the lamp stands decorating the tabernacle were made of almond wood. The tree was also a source of almond oil and food.

Cedar trees were mentioned frequently in the Old Testament (1 Kings 6:9, Job 40:17, Psalm 92:12, and Ezekiel 27:5). They were a source of wood for the temple Solomon built for the Lord, the masts of ships, and many other things. The cedars of Lebanon were once in abundance in the Mediterranean area, but they're now scarce.

The *citrus tree* produced the fruit used in the Jewish Feast of Tabernacles and was considered a tree "worth its weight in gold." It's referred to in the New International Version of the Bible in Revelation 18:11-12, where it says, "The merchants of the earth will weep and mourn over her (speaking about the city of Babylon) because no one buys their cargos any more - cargoes of gold, silver, precious stones and pearls; fine linen, purple, silk and scarlet cloth; every sort of *citron wood* (emphasis added), and articles of every kind made of ivory, costly wood, bronze, iron and marble…"

The *cypress tree* or *gopher wood* was a tall pyramidal-shaped tree with a hard, durable reddish hued wood. It was used in the building of the ark and other things (Genesis 6:14 with an additional reference in Isaiah 41: 19 and 60:13).

The *fig tree* was a bush-like tree producing edible fruits that became known as "the poor man's food" because fig trees were so plentiful in the countries of the Mediterranean that everyone could eat of the fruit of that tree. The fig tree was the first plant mentioned in the Bible (Genesis 3:7). It represented peace and prosperity (1 Kings 4:25, Micah 4:4, and Zechariah 3:10).

The *olive tree* was named or alluded to nearly 80 times in the Bible. The tree, itself, was referred to in the New Testament in Romans 11:13-27. There, Paul was speaking to the Gentiles when he told them that they were like "wild olive shoots" who have been grafted into God's chosen group of people "to share the richness of the olive tree." But, he goes on to say that Gentiles ought not to boast of that because they do not support the root, but rather the root supports them. The faith of Gentiles has allowed God to graft them in!

The Mount of Olives was mentioned in both the Old and New Testaments (2 Samuel 15:30 and Acts 1:12). It was so named because of the olive groves that covered it in ancient times. The "Mount" was actually four flattened and rounded summits that the people from the city of Jerusalem went to in the hope of escaping heat from a crowded city. The Kidron Valley, on the western side, was often the place where sheep grazed among the olive trees and, also on the western side above the Kidron Valley, was where the Garden of Gethsemane was believed to have been located.

From the direction of the Mount of Olives came Jesus Christ as He approached the city of Jerusalem on His triumphal entry when crowds gathered and spread palm branches on the street to welcome Him (Luke 19:28-38).

141

"...he went on ahead, going up to Jerusalem. When he drew near to Bethphage and Bethany, at the mount that is called Olivet, he sent two of the disciples, saying, 'Go into the village opposite, where on entering you will find a colt tied, on which no one has ever yet sat; untie it and bring it here. If any one asks you, Why are you untying it? you shall say this, The Lord has need of it.' So those who were sent went away and found it as he had told them. And as they were untying the colt, its owners said to them, 'Why are you untying the colt?' And they said, 'The Lord has need of it.' And they brought it to Jesus, and throwing their garments on the colt they set Jesus upon it. And as he rode along, they spread their garments on the road. As he was now drawing near, at the descent of the Mount of Olives, the whole multitude of the disciples began to rejoice and praise God with a loud voice for all the mighty works that they had seen, saying, 'Blessed is the King who comes in the name of the Lord! Peace in heaven and glory in the highest!'"

Finally, the *palm tree* was another tree of importance. It was used in the Jewish Feast of the Tabernacles (Leviticus 23:40 and Nehemiah 8:15).

Prayer:
Oh Lord, help me this day to pick from the tree of knowledge information that will help me understand what's

expected of me and what You want me to accomplish this day. Just as trees grow upwards, but also sink new roots deeper into the ground in search of life-giving moisture, help me to grow spiritually by sinking new roots deeper into You, O Lord. Help me to be "rooted and grounded" in You, O Lord, so that when the winds of adversity or raging storms come my way I am able to weather them. I pray for strength and guidance in meeting the problems I may face this day…so that, like those bent, gnarled, rough trees growing above timberline in the mountains, I will persevere and survive to see another day, tomorrow. Help me to grow in the knowledge that life, and the life hereafter, holds many rewards for those who seek Your will and keep their sights on You.

Amen

Devotional Reading #19

Boats

In Biblical times, boats often played an important role. In the Old Testament, in the book of Genesis, Chapter 6, you can read the familiar story about Noah building the ark. In John 6:16-24, in the New Testament, is found the equally familiar story about Jesus coming into the boat of the disciples while their boat was being tossed about by a raging storm.

But, less familiar is the story of Apostle Paul being shipwrecked off the coast of Malta. In Acts 27-28, we read about the journey of Paul that ended in a disastrous shipwreck. Briefly, the story goes like this: Paul was being taken to Rome to stand trial before Caesar because a group of Jews had reported that Paul had spoken out against them and their law. As they were going toward the island of Crete, en route to Rome, a strong wind came up and raged for three days and nights. Everyone on board feared for their lives, but Paul told them that an angel of God had told him that, although the ship would be wrecked, none of them would lose their lives.

After two weeks of drifting across the sea of Adria, they suspected that they were near land, so about midnight they "sounded" and found that they were at twenty fathoms. A little farther on they sounded again and found that they were at fifteen fathoms. Afraid that the boat would crash into the rocks, they let out four anchors from the stern, and prayed for the day to come. There were 276 people on board the ship.

When morning came they noticed they weren't far from a bay with a beach. They made for the beach, but the boat hit a shoal; the bow stuck and remained immovable, and the stern was broken up by the surf. They were, indeed, shipwrecked!

Since there were prisoners on board (of which Paul was one) many of the guards wanted to kill the prisoners, but the centurion, wishing to save Paul's life, kept them from carrying out that act.

He ordered everyone who could swim to throw themselves overboard first and make for the land, while the rest were to make for the land on pieces of the ship that they could find and use for that purpose.

Thus, it was as Paul had said, the ship was lost, but no one lost their life. You can read the rest of this great story in Acts 28.

Dear reader, three Biblical stories were cited here, (1) the building of the ark by Noah, (2) Jesus walking on the waters as He came to His disciples in the boat, and (3) Paul being shipwrecked near Malta. I'm sure many lessons might be learned from these three stories, but one of the lessons that stands out for me is the fact that (a) *Noah heard the voice of God with instructions to build the ark,* (b) *Paul heard the voice of one of God's angels in the midst of the storm telling him 'Do not be afraid, Paul,'* and (c) *Jesus said to his disciples, "Why are you afraid, O men of little faith?" And, then He arose and rebuked the winds and the sea; and there was a great calm.*

God was clearly in charge of each of those three situations!

And, what about you, dear reader? Have you ever been in a boat when a storm raged about you? Were you frightened? Did you cry out to God for help? What were the circumstances?

I can certainly tell you that I was in such a circumstance once and I was scared stiff! Terrified might be a better word! I was on a canoe trip in the Boundary Waters along the United States-Canadian Boarder when winds came up and whipped the waters into white caps! With three canoes in our group, each canoe was pretty well loaded with either supplies or people. The waves lapped at the sides of the canoes and with each roll of the waves I thought we were going to capsize. Water flowed into the canoes with each breaker and if there were three people in the canoe, the "duffer" began bailing the water out of the bottom of the canoe with whatever container was available. I prayed right out loud, "O Lord, help us, we are going to capsize! Help us make it to shore!"

The prayers were heard, God answered, and we made it safely to the shore...all three canoes!

Later on in life I got a job *cleaning* boats! Yes! Cleaning them! The showroom floor was full of cruisers and speed boats and my job was to clean them! Have you ever tried, by hand, to wash a cruiser? Well, I'd never done that before either, but I got a bucket of sudsy water, a scrub brush, a ladder and went to work. Funny how looking at that cruiser, it didn't look that big, but washing it...well...it *was* big! And then I set to work vacuuming the inside...way down inside the front of the boat... the "bow" of the boat. I went so far inside the bow of that boat that daylight was marginal and I could barely see what I was doing. Nevertheless, I finally got that water-craft clean and then tackled speed boats, row boats, and canoes. Ultimately, I had all of the boats in the showroom clean and since I never "dawdled or wasted time or even took a break" I was done with time to spare! I'd been sent there from a temporary job placement service and if I didn't fill up the forty hours of work for that week, I wouldn't get the full pay, so I grabbed the vacuum and began cleaning the entire showroom. I moved furniture that hadn't been moved in years and cleaned behind and underneath it and finally, at the end of the week, the owner of the establishment said he wanted to hire me full time as he'd never seen anyone work so hard with such a degree of commitment! I thought about it, but decided that I hadn't spent four years getting a college education and a degree to end up washing boats for a living! Thus ended my "sudsy career with boats!"

Prayer:
Oh, Lord, Your Holy Word says in 1 Chronicles 16: 11, *"Seek the Lord and his strength, seek his presence continually."* On this day, wherever I may go or whatever I may do…when there are storms all around me and I am adrift in life, help me to seek You and to receive Your strength and protection. Be with me continually, O Lord! Be my "helmsman" and guide me through the turbulent waters. Help me to avoid being swamped, capsized or shipwrecked this day. Bring me through the shoals and treacherous rocks and help me reach the day's end…safely! This I ask in your precious name, Jesus.

Amen

Devotional Reading #20

Jobs

In the Bible, in Colossians 3:23-25, it says, *"Whatever your task, knowing that from the Lord you will receive the inheritance as your reward; you are serving the Lord Christ."*

Dear reader, as you reflect back on the jobs you've had during your lifetime, what comes to mind? Can you remember your first job? Can you remember how it posed new challenges for you? Was it a job that required special schooling? Or was it a job that you learned as you performed it…through on-the-job-training? Did you like your first job? Were you employed at it for very long? What were the circumstances of your first job? Keep your first job in mind as you read the following accounts.

Following my first interview for a teaching job, I was flown, at the expense of the Menominee School District, to Michigan to "see what the job entailed." The Superintendent of Schools met me at the airport and ushered me into his car. I thought it a little strange that the first place he took me to was the little city park, but I said nothing and tried to sound excited and impressed with the couple of deer they had there…cooped up inside a small zoo area! I smiled and kept asking him all sorts of questions about the town, school, community and whatever else I could think to ask questions about. Thus, ultimately, we got to the school where I was to teach eighth grade American History and General Science, should I decide to accept the job.

"What?" I exclaimed, "you want me to teach General Science? I can't teach that...I've only got a Biology minor...that means I've only had classes in Zoology and Botany. I can't teach General Science!"

"Oh," he said, "I'm completely confident that you can teach General Science and do a fine job, at that!"

So, it wasn't long before I had moved to the Upper Peninsula of Michigan, found a small apartment and, at the age of twenty-two, began my first teaching job.

Of course, first year teaching jobs are always a challenge! There are daily lesson plans, units of study to consider, names of students to learn, and a whole host of new experiences for the beginning teacher!

I had 5 classes of eighth graders with one of the classes containing 35 students. That class was a "sea of faces," virtually "wall-to-wall kids" as I stood up in front and tried to get everyone arranged alphabetically so I could learn their names. Passing out textbooks and getting everyone's book number recorded, setting up seating charts, taking roll and trying to get to know the students was a difficult task. But, on the second day, I noticed a little fellow standing in the back of the room. He was as tall standing as the other kids were seated, and in that "sea of faces" he had blended in, completely. Nevertheless, on that day I asked him if he wouldn't please sit down so class could start. He said, "Miss Daniels, I'd like to sit down, but there's no place for me to sit. There are no more desks and I've been standing back here for two days now!"

Oh, my gosh! Well, so a desk was borrowed from another room and all was finally well for the little guy!

In that same class of students was another little guy I'll never forget. Bradley would come into that American History class carrying his brief case and he *knew* his American History, let me tell you!

Now, I often liked to...well..."embellish" some of the American History stories that were in the students' textbooks. I loved to "really get into the telling of those stories!" I figured that way maybe the students would remember the events better. My evenings were spent poring over library books that told more and went deeper than the information found in their textbooks. That was the information I embellished the stories with and told to the students. Once in awhile, however, I'd get completely carried away and…well…go a little too far in the telling.

At that point it never failed, that little guy, Bradley, would raise his hand, and I'd know…oh, oh, I'd gone too far. But, I'd call on little Bradley, he'd get up from his desk, snap to attention, and say, "Miss Daniels, I don't think that's quite correct." And, then, he'd proceed to tell the *real story*! Oh, it was great! I loved it! I knew the little guy was an American History buff and so, not only did the class get a history lesson, but his teacher did too! It was great!

I've often wondered whatever happened to little Bradley and whether he went into politics or became a lawyer. He had what it took! He was a gem!

Another class had "Frank," and Frank was a diplomat from the word "go!" It was in his blood! Frank would observe how this new, young teacher responded to questions asked. If it appeared that I wasn't sure how to answer a question, or perhaps didn't know the answer to a question, Frank's hand would shoot up, instantly. I'd call on him and then he'd say something like, "Well, Miss Daniels, I think the correct answer might be…(whatever fit) or he'd say, a possibility might be…(whatever)." He gave me time to think…time to phrase my answer in such a way that it was plausible and maybe even correct. Many a time, 'ole Frank "saved the day" for me as a first year teacher. He was a life saver!

One day, in that same class, which met just before lunchtime, the students were all busy at their desks with an assignment. I was seated at my desk in the front of the room. It was so quiet you could hear a pin drop. Suddenly, I smelled it! There was no mistaking it, that odor was unmistakable. Someone was eating an orange!

Looking up, I said, "all right, whoever's eating that orange, bring it up here and lay it on the corner of the desk!"

So, from the very last desk by the back wall of the room a fellow came forward and placed his orange on the desk. He said, "How did you know I was eating it?" And, I said, "Because I smelled it!" He was astonished, to say the least, and I told him, "Don't ever do it again…even if it is right before lunchtime and you're hungry!"

That first year teaching I met another first year teacher who taught ninth and tenth grade Math. We became friends and she told me a funny story about how one morning it had rained when the kids had had to come to school. In those days, before all of the busing that's popular nowadays, kids walked to school. And, so, on that particular day by the time the kids got to school many of them were wet. Their clothes were wet. As Kay, the Math teacher, had given her class a book assignment, everyone was quietly busy. She was busy at her desk when she smelled something unpleasant. She looked up to see that the students had tied the cords of the window shades together from one end of the room to nearly the other end, above the radiators, and there they'd hung up their socks to dry!

Thus, dear reader, as regards our first jobs...we learned by doing them. We may have had special training for those first jobs, but inevitably we learned by actually doing the job and many valuable lessons were learned on those "first jobs."

In Matthew 20:1-16, we read about some workers who went to work in a vineyard. The story is one of the parables that Jesus spoke to His disciples. The ultimate objective of this parable was made clear to the disciples...that in the final analysis, it's not what jobs or tasks we've performed, or even how well we've performed them that's important...it's how we've related to Jesus, the Son of man.

Here is the parable: *"For the kingdom of heaven is like a householder who went out early in the morning to hire laborers for his vineyard. After agreeing with the laborers for a denarius a day, he sent them into his vineyard. And going out about the third hour he saw others standing idle in the marketplace; and to them he said, 'You go into the vineyard too, and whatever is right I will give you.' So they went. Going out again about the sixth hour and the ninth hour, he did the same. And about the eleventh hour he went out and found others standing; and he said to them, 'Why do you stand here idle all day?' They said to him, 'Because no one has hired us,' He said to them, 'You go into the vineyard too.' And when evening came, the owner of the vineyard said to his steward, 'Call the laborers and pay them their wages, beginning with the last, up to the first.' And when those hired about the eleventh hour came, they thought they would receive more but each of them also received a denarius. And on receiving it they grumbled at the householder, saying, 'These last worked only one hour, and you have made them equal to us who have borne the burden of the day and the scorching heat. But he replied to one of them, 'Friend, I am doing you no wrong; did you not agree with me for a denarius? Take what belongs to you, and go; I choose to give to this last as I give to you. Am I not allowed to do what I choose with what belongs to me? Or do you begrudge my generosity? So the last will be first, and the first last."'*

I believe, dear reader, that this parable illustrates that, as Christians, it's not what we do for the Lord...what our work consists of...nor how long we do it that's important to Him. It's *why* we're doing it. We should be doing it simply because we *know and love Jesus*; because He resides in our heart! We cannot pile up "brownie points" with Him by the work we do!

In Matthew 19:28-30, it says, *"Jesus said to them, 'Truly, I say to you, in the new world, when the Son of man shall sit on his glorious throne, you who have followed me will also sit on twelve thrones, judging the twelve tribes of Israel. And every one who has left houses or brothers or sisters or father or mother or children or lands, for my name's sake, will receive a hundredfold, and inherit eternal life. But many that are first will be last and the last first.'"*

Thus, in the parable of the workers in the vineyard, the workers who went into the field last were paid first and those who'd worked in the field all day were paid last. All workers were paid the same amount of money because they'd all agreed to work in the field for a denarius.

Thus, it is with us as Christians. When we die and go before the Lord and He reviews the work we've done over the course of our lives...those things we've done of a Christian nature...*it's our hearts that he'll look at!* He'll look to see if we did those deeds *because we knew and loved Him*, no other reason! If He deems that's why we did those tasks, then eternal life will be our reward. It isn't important how many years we've sung in the church choir, it isn't important how much money we've contributed to the church, it isn't how many poor people we've helped, it isn't important how long we've been a Christian, etc., *it's how well we've known and loved Jesus that's important!*

Prayer:
Oh, heavenly Father, please increase in me a greater love for You. I've asked You into my life as my Lord and Savior, but I want to know You better and love You more. I want You to be on the "throne of my life" overseeing all that I do in my life so that when I'm called before You I can hear the words, *"Well done good and faithful servant; you have been faithful over a little; I will set you over much, enter into the joy of your master."*

Amen

Refining and Testing With Fire

As a first year General Science teacher, one of the experiments I performed taught me, quite literally, about "being refined and tested with fire!"

I was a Biology minor and yet I was hired to teach General Science. When I saw the student textbook I knew that my job was going to be doubly challenging as the book was hopelessly out of date, the pictures were 1940 vintage! And so, I chose units of study that I thought the students ought to know about and spent long hours each evening reading and preparing for the next day's lesson.

At one point I tackled the subject of Geology and I found an experiment in a library book that told how to make "molten iron." Well, never having performed the experiment before I read the directions carefully, tried to memorize what I read and figured it must be a lot like "making a cake"…just follow the directions, use the right ingredients, and voila! Molten iron!

So, the next day in class, I spread a piece of asbestos (it was in the days before we knew about the dangers of asbestos!) on the desktop in front of my classroom. Then,

I put some of the necessary powder on the asbestos, forming about a four inch high mound, and finally, the ignition powder on top of that and, poised to step backward quickly, I lit it with a match! A brief pause and then...*BAM!...THE THING EXPLODED WITH A TUMULTUOUS NOISE!* Instantly, the whole room of kids jumped to their feet...eyes as big as saucers! "Wow! What an experiment," they said, "cool!"

But I have to tell you...I got molten iron! No doubt about that! There it was...right there inside that black hollowed out crater that had burned into the desktop! It had burned right through the sheet of asbestos and created a black crater in the desktop! Also, for a few brief moments I'd had to stamp out fires from a few pieces that had flown off and landed on the floor! No doubt about it, it was an exciting experiment, one that I bet the kids in that General Science class remember to this day!

"Refining" means "being improved or perfected." I guess you could say that...personally and quite literally...I had learned about being "refined and tested with fire" in that experiment! As a first year teacher I was fortunate that no one (including myself) had gotten hurt or that I hadn't set the school on fire!

(As a side note to that story, I have to tell you, dear reader, I only stayed one year at that school in Michigan before I went home to Minnesota. Not that I was fired over that "desktop crater" or anything, I just wanted to go back to Minnesota. There, I taught in two more school districts before I quit teaching and went into industry where I worked for a Fortune 500 company as a technical writer, procedures writer and ultimately, a National Product Planner. It was at that company that I met John Poulos, who became my husband.)

And, now, back to this devotional reading and how this subject of "refining and testing with fire" might relate to you, the reader, Christian living and the Bible...

In the Bible, the first letter of Peter was directed to the Christians scattered in what is modern day Turkey, but the message in 1 Peter 1:3-9 might very well be for modern day Christians everywhere. *"Blessed be the God and Father of our Lord Jesus Christ! By His great mercy we have been born anew to a living hope through the resurrection of Jesus Christ from the dead, and to an inheritance which is imperishable, undefiled, and unfading, kept in heaven for you, who by God's power are guarded through faith for a salvation ready to be revealed in the last time. In this you rejoice, though now for a little while you may have to suffer various trials, so that the genuineness of your faith, more precious than gold which, though perishable, is tested by fire, may redound to praise and glory and honor at the revelation of Jesus*

Christ. Without having seen Him you love Him and rejoice with unutterable and exalted joy. As the outcome of your faith you obtain the salvation of your souls."

Those verses point out that because of what Jesus Christ did for us when He died on the cross, we have salvation and have been born anew "to a living hope through his resurrection from the dead." Nevertheless, now, for a little while, we may have to suffer various trials. Some of the trials will test the genuineness of our faith and some of the trials might, figuratively speaking, *"take us through the fire"*...they may be quite serious and taxing trials.

The question is: how deep does our faith go? Is it enough to get us through the *"refining and testing?"*

In Jeremiah 9:7, it says, *"Therefore thus says the Lord of hosts; 'Behold, I will refine them and test them...'"* And, in Isaiah 48:10, it says: *"Behold, I have refined you, but not like silver, I have tried you in the furnace of affliction."*

In Psalm 66:10-12, we're told: *"For thou, O God, has tried us; thou hast tried us as silver is tried."*
Sometimes, because we are 100% human, we may find ourselves in some sort of situation that causes us hardship and pain. God could, if He wanted to, give us a life free

of pain and hardships, but our faith, it's sad to say, would not grow and deepen as much as when our lives encompass a certain amount of trouble. It's during the times of trouble that we often cry out to God for whatever we need. Maybe we need a healing or maybe we're suffering in a relationship that needs altering or mending, maybe we need a job, money, or a place to live; there might be any number of situations that we need help with and which cause us to seek the Lord at that time.

In Hebrews 12:11, it says, *"For the moment all discipline seems painful rather than pleasant; later it yields the peaceful fruit of righteousness to those who have been trained by it."*

When we come *"through the fire"* and we've been *"refined and tested"* to a greater degree, we can praise the Lord! Whatever the outcome, it is all gain if we "hold fast to the Lord Jesus Christ!"

And that is the message of this devotional reading, dear reader: hold fast to the Lord Jesus Christ through your times of *refining and testing with fire!* In Matthew 6:34, it says, *"Therefore do not be anxious about tomorrow, for tomorrow will be anxious for itself. Let the day's own trouble be sufficient for the day."*

And, in 2 Corinthians 12:8-10, Paul tells about a thorn in his flesh. He says, *"Three times I besought the Lord about this, that it should leave me; but he said to me, 'My grace is sufficient for you, for my power is made perfect in weakness.' I will all the more gladly boast of my weaknesses, that the power of Christ may rest upon me. For the sake of Christ, then, I am content with weaknesses, insults, hardships, persecutions, and calamities; for when I am weak, then I am strong."*

Prayer:
Oh, Lord Jesus, help me to hold fast to you when life presents me with times of refining and testing. Whatever the situation that I find myself in…help me to come through it because you are with me. Nothing else matters except that you are with me, Lord Jesus. Take me successfully through life's "refining and testings with fire" and bring me to the other side. Help me to remember that your ways are sufficient for me.

Amen

Devotional Reading #22

Love is Patient and Kind, Love is...

In 1 Corinthians 13:4-7, it says, *"Love is patient and kind; love is not jealous or boastful; it is not arrogant or rude. Love does not insist on its own way; it is not irritable or resentful, it does not rejoice at wrong, but rejoices in the right. Love bears all things, believes all things, hopes all things, endures all things."*

And in 1 Corinthians 13:13, we read, *"So faith, hope, love abide, these three; but the greatest of these is love."*

Dear reader, did anyone come to mind as you read those verses? What person or persons in your life have you loved the most? How deep did that love go?

When I was twenty seven years old, I once thought if I could have a man respect, be attentive to, and date me for even six months that I would be ever so grateful to God! I even prayed to that end, hoping that God would grant me such a blessing.

And, when such a man did materialize and was a factor in my life for six months before he exited, I thought God had heard my prayer and answered it...I was prepared to be content the rest of my life with the memories of the man's attentiveness and kindnesses toward me. I dared not hope there'd be anyone else!

Nevertheless, when I was 33, the place of my employment provided an opportunity to meet a "confirmed bachelor by the name of John" who was 39. John had a policy that he'd never date any gal from the place he worked, so I figured I had a slim chance of getting a date with him. Ultimately, however, he gave in and with both of us "head over heals in love," we were married in 1974.

John and I honeymooned in Hawaii. We landed in Honolulu and then boarded a small commuter plane headed for the island of Kawai. When we touched down in Kawai, John was out of that plane like a shot, grabbed my hand, and away we went! He was on a mission to get that rental car and be on our way! Clutching my purse and carry-on bag as best I could, I got in the car and was soon whizzing down the highway, sixty miles an hour!

I said, "Ah, John, why are you in such a hurry? This is an island and we've got plenty of time, we're going to be here awhile."

He responded with, "Yes, I know, but I want to see the island!"

"I know, so do I," I responded, "but we didn't even wait to get our suitcases! They're still being unloaded from the plane!"

"Oh, we can get them later," he said. "Let's just get going!"

Well, I have to tell you...since we were on our honeymoon, I didn't know if he was in that big a hurry to see the island or get to the motel!

Nevertheless, the week progressed nicely and we had a wonderful time on Kawai. But, when it came time to leave, I began to wonder about another "mission" he seemed to be on. This time he wanted to "catch a few more rays of sunshine" before the commuter plane left to take us back to Honolulu, so I said I'd "nose around" in the airport gift shop while he sunbathed. Nevertheless, something got fouled up because all of a sudden they announced that our flight was leaving.

Oh, my gosh, where was John? I searched everywhere, calling as I ran! He was nowhere to be found and so...that flight left without us! Well, I have to tell you, by the time I found him there was steam coming out of my ears! I was fit to be tied! About that time I was seriously wondering what sort of a fellow I'd married.

John, however, remained calm, cool, and… sunburned, and said there'd be another commuter plane along shortly as they ran between the islands all the time. As it turned out, he was right and we returned to Honolulu where we completed a wonderful honeymoon in paradise!

Afterwards, back home, married life proved to have its challenges for John! Ever the helpful husband, one time John decided he'd do the laundry and help out his working wife.

It had been some time since I'd seen my favorite blue sweater and so I asked John if he'd seen it lately. Without much said, he disappeared into the basement and came back with a four by five inch blue sweater! It looked like something a year-old baby would wear!

"What's that?" I asked. "Is that my favorite blue sweater? Gosh, what did you do to it?"

Well, of course, he'd washed and dried it along with all the other clothes, not knowing that I planned to wash it separately. At any rate, that was the end of that favorite sweater!

One other time I had given him directions to put the casserole dish I'd pre-made for supper into the oven, as I had to work late that night. When I came home I found that he'd broiled it! He *broiled* the hot dish! It was burned on top and raw underneath! (Gosh, don't men *know* what to do with casserole dishes? I was amazed!)

As I write this, John and I have been married over thirty years. Nevertheless, we know a couple who celebrated their seventy-first wedding anniversary last summer. Can you imagine being married to the same person for seventy-one years? And yet, all around us we hear of friends, acquaintances and relatives who are divorced or who are contemplating it; there are many reasons for the breakups. Every situation is different, every couple, unique.

If you, dear reader, are a single person, someone who has either never married, or who has been married and now isn't, try to apply what follows to a relationship with someone you have loved or do currently love…perhaps it's a parent or a friend.

Contemplate the word "love." Let's read again the verses that appeared at the beginning of this devotion. Look carefully at each of the words in those verses as they relate to the word "Love."

Love is…*patient*…(What does it mean to be "patient" with someone? Can you think of a time in your life when you were particularly patient with someone whom you loved…you went through some sort of a trial?)

Love is patient and *kind* (did you show kindness while you were being patient? Could you have shown more kindness than you did show?)

Love is *not jealous or boastful* (jealousy is so divisive a quality, it will destroy most relationships. And, rather than being a braggart and being boastful, strive toward humility, instead.)

Love is *not arrogant or rude* (arrogance and rudeness will get you nowhere.)

Love does *not insist on its own way* (when love abounds, flexibility and yielding to the other person's desires readily occurs.)

Love is *not irritable or resentful* (peacefulness in heart and actions, plus not letting the other person's words or actions cause you ill will should be your goal.)

Love does *not rejoice at wrong, but rejoices in the right.* (When good things happen to your loved one, you rejoice!)

Love *bears all things, believes all things, hopes all things, endures all things.* (Feelings of love toward the other person are all positive in nature.) While thirty years of marriage doesn't make for an expert on the subject of love, nevertheless, here are some beliefs and practices that might make for heightened love with another person.

1) Strive to really "listen" to what your loved one is saying to you. Notice the *way* something is said to you and what body language is being used. Too often we're so caught up in speaking that we don't listen and aren't observant! Give your loved one your undivided attention when they're speaking to you. Too many people let their own personal thoughts, interests, problems, etc., crowd out the communication that's being directed toward them.

2) Realize that the loved one is entitled to their opinion, even if it's diametrically opposite your opinion. Someone once told me, "no one owns another person." A loved one is a distinctly different person, and love will strive to accept those differences!

3) When love has, for the moment, worn thin in a relationship, declare a "time out," a "cooling off period" and put some distance between you and your loved one. A walk would be good.

4) Try to never let the sun set on a day, never let the day end, but what disagreements have been resolved (at least to some degree).

5) Regardless of what the disagreement, the words "I'm sorry" will have to be spoken by one person in the relationship. If neither person is able to do that, love will suffer.

6) A love relationship requires "working together" to make it a success. Common goals will foster and heighten a love relationship.

7) It's important that you "love yourself" and keep yourself looking attractive to those around you. Often times a new hairdo or some new clothes will heighten your loved one's attentiveness and attraction. Remember, when you accept and love yourself, those around you find it easier to love you!

This list could go on and on as many things could be said about "love." Love relationships must be "worked on," they don't succeed and endure the test of time easily.

A recipe for a successful love relationship might go something like this: Measure a cup of friendship and thoughtfulness, cream together with a pinch of powdered tenderness, beat very lightly in a bowl of love with a generous cup of faith and hope. Next add a spoonful of gaiety and laughter, moistened with sudden tears of heartfelt sympathy and bake in a pan at home temperature. Serve often in the hopes that it will emanate serenity, beauty, faith, discipline and an awareness of the brotherhood of mankind, the sonship of Jesus Christ, and the Fatherhood of God Almighty. (Thanks to Mr. J. Tearse of Winona, MN, for portions of this poem.)

Prayer:
Oh, Heavenly Father, help me to remember that You loved the world so much that You sent your only begotten son, Jesus Christ, into this world to perish and die on the cross that we might have eternal life. You sent Jesus not to condemn the world, but to, through Him, offer salvation to the world. What love Jesus exhibited when He agreed to die on that cross for us and our sins! It's as if Jesus was asked, "How much do you love them?" and He stretched out His arms and hands and said ...this much...and then He died! Work in us, oh Lord, to increase our love for the people in our daily lives and the people we come in contact with... to strive for such love as You had for us.

Amen

Leaven, Lumps and Dross

In 1 Corinthians 5:6-8, we read, *"...Do you not know that a little leaven (yeast) leavens (permeates) the whole lump? Cleanse out the old leaven that you may be a new lump, as you really are unleavened. For Christ, our paschal lamb, has been sacrificed. Let us, therefore, celebrate the festival, not with the old leaven, the leaven of malice and evil, but with the unleavened bread of sincerity and truth."*

And, in Proverbs 25:4-5, it says, *"Take away the dross from the silver, and the smith has material for a vessel; take away the wicked from the presence of the king, and his throne will be established in righteousness."*

One day in our house, the basement drain was plugged up. John got a coil of wire called a "snake" and, projecting it into the drain, tried to unplug whatever it was that was causing the water to back up. No luck! Ultimately, he had no choice but to call in "the man." He came with his expert plumbing equipment and tried to dislodge the stopped-up drain. Again, no luck!

With finality, the plumber said that his heavy duty plumbing equipment should have done the job! He couldn't imagine what was lodged *so tightly* that even his expert plumbing equipment failed to dislodge it! He said there was only one thing to do and that was to jack-hammer through the floor tiles, jack-hammer through the cement floor, break it up, cut the pipe near the problem area and then he would know what the problem was! Well, I have to tell you, as I stood there listening to "the man" and looking at John's face, I could see dollar signs ringing up in John's eyes! There was *no way* he was going to pay for the man to come in there, jack-hammer the floor tiles, jack-hammer the cement floor, break it up, cut the pipe near the problem area, find out what the problem was, and then replace the cut pipe with new pipe, re-cement the floor and replace the floor tiles! Absolutely *no way* was John going to pay all that money to the man!

And, so it was that, within the hour, I found myself in our car speeding away from a rental shop with a rented jack-hammer in the trunk headed back to our house!

Had we ever used a jack-hammer before? Had *either* of us ever earnestly *watched* anyone use a jack-hammer before? *Nope!* Did we have even the faintest idea of how to do this job? *Nope*, not a clue!

Well, I have to tell you, John plugged that jack-hammer in, turned it on, and, with John holding onto the jack-hammer (that powerful beast!) for all he was worth, and me holding on to John for all I was worth…we jack-hammered through the floor tiles and cement floor, right down to that piping buried beneath the basement floor! We took turns sawing the pipe with a hack saw and a few other saws and ultimately we found "the culprit." We found out what the problem was!

Over the years "lead slag" that they'd used to join the extensions of pipe together had acted as a "stoppage point" for other sediments that had built up there, much like arteries in the human body clog up with plaque. The opening had gotten smaller and smaller, gradually solidified, and finally, no water could go through the pipe.

So, proud of ourselves that we'd found the culprit, John put down new piping, new floor cement, and finally new floor tiling. We'd done the job ourselves and saved "tons" of money doing it!

Nevertheless, the job wasn't finished at that point, because now the new floor tiles were all bright and shiny and the rest of the basement floor looked dingy and dirty, by comparison. *So*…back to the rental shop we went and before long we'd rented a heavy duty floor scrubber/buffer! And, with John holding onto that heavy duty floor scrubber/buffer and me holding onto John, around the basement we went! We scrubbed, then waxed, and finally buffed that entire basement floor…together…in tandem! And when it was all over with…we sat on the basement steps and said, "Not bad…not bad! And, we did the job ourselves!"

Dear reader, all that work was needed just to get rid of a little "lead slag and dross" that had built up in the pipe. So it is with our lives. We go along living our daily lives and sometimes we're engaged in things that we shouldn't be doing. And, then, ultimately, those things, over the years, get added to and first thing you know…we're overly anxious, afraid, bitter, defeated, depressed, discouraged, doubtful, sick, sorrowful, weary or worried, to name only a few things, all of a negative nature. A little bit of "slag" in our lives has been added to by more "dross" that came along and ultimately, we suffer.

What about you, dear reader, what's bothering you today? What area of your life is not what it should be or could be today? Can you explain *why* that area is bothering you?

Whatever your problem is, dear reader, meditate this day on the words in 1 Corinthians 5: 6-8 and Proverbs 25:4-5. They talk about leaven (which might also be called "yeast"), lumps, and dross. The old leaven of "malice and evil" ought to be replaced with an unleavened bread of "sincerity and truth." In other words, the things in our lives that we've engaged in in the past, be they thoughts, beliefs, or actions (some with malice and evil) weren't good for us. They need to be rooted out and gotten rid of so that our lives might be better (filled with sincerity and truth).

And, as it says in Proverbs 25:4-5, if the dross is taken away from the silver then the "smith," i.e., Christ, has material for a vessel. Take away the wicked from the presence of the king and his throne will be established in righteousness.

Prayer:
Cleanse me, O Lord, from the old leavens I've carried around with me over past years…leavens that are not good for me and that may have caused me _____
(write in the area of your life you'd like changed). Bring to mind in the course of this day…ways that I can change. Help me to get rid of the old leavens, help me to get rid of the dross, O Lord. And, replace those areas in my life with new, fresh, live leavens that can help me to become a new vessel that You, O Lord, can shape into Your image.

Amen

Open Phone Lines

In John 10:3-5, we read, *"...the gatekeeper opens; the sheep hear his voice, and he calls his own sheep by name and leads them out. When he has brought out all his own, he goes before them, and the sheep follow him, and they know his voice. A stranger they will not follow, but they will flee from him, for they do not know the voice of strangers."*

When married, living in our first home and in need of saving money wherever possible, John came up with the idea of having a "telephone party line" installed. It was the 1970's and it seemed like a brilliant idea, as hardly anyone had a party line any more. John called the telephone company and they assured him that, yes, we could have a party line and at a really cheap monthly rate! When word got around where we worked that we had a telephone party line, one of our co-workers poked fun at us and said he thought we probably had the only party line in all of St. Paul! Being laughed at didn't bother us, and for many years we enjoyed the use of a "private" party line at a really low monthly rate. Everything went along just fine until one day we picked up the phone and someone was already talking! A little old lady had been added to our party line…a little old lady who *loved* to talk on the telephone! She was *always* on the phone and we'd have to ask her if we could use the phone. It made for an awkward situation. Thus, because of her we had to cancel out of the party line and install a private line; I guess you could say "we went modern." With the private line installed it seemed to be a signal to John, he began installing phones everywhere! He installed three on the first floor of our home, three on the second floor, two in the basement and a telephone in the garage, for a total of *eight* telephones! Talk about going from one extreme to the other!

Ironically, even though we had eight telephones, we had only one incoming phone line, so just one phone could be used at a time! The other seven phones just sat there "waiting their turn" until either John or I chose them for an incoming call. An "open line" existed for all eight phones until a particular phone receiver was picked up, making the connection complete!

A lot of people wonder why, when they've prayed to God, they don't seem to "get an answer." They don't feel that God heard their prayers. They've felt that "the connection" wasn't completed for some reason, and sometimes they lose heart and give up.

Part of the reason is because, as it says in John 10: 14, "I am the good shepherd; I know my own and my own know me" and in John 10:27, *"My sheep hear my voice and I know them, and they follow me."* Many times we have only ourselves to blame because we've not spent enough time with "the shepherd." We don't really know Him, only *of* Him! Ours is not a personal knowledge of Him or a personal relationship with Him.

It's like those eight phone lines…when the phone rings, maybe we know the person at the other end of the line, and maybe we don't. If the person has never called us before or only does so once in a while, we don't know them. Maybe we know *of* that person, but we don't know them personally.

Prayer time with "the good shepherd" ought to be done, daily. It ought to be a specific time set aside for being with Him and prayers need to be more than just a "grocery list" of what we want from Him.

Prayers ought to involve *praising* Him. (Praise Him for who He is and what He's done for mankind when He died on that cross of salvation. Tell Him you love Him.)

Prayers ought to involve *thanking* Him. (Thank Him for all sorts of things. Name them. Tell Him what things you've received that have made you happy, i.e., the sunshine of a new day, life, home, friends, loved ones, whatever).

Prayers ought to involve *petitions.* (Petition Him with prayers for the country, its leaders, world situations, local situations, and for people who are ill…and name them).

Prayer time ought to involve *reading His Word, the Bible.* Strive to saturate your mind with verses and lessons found in the Bible. The Bible is a letter to you…from God's heart…to yours. You don't have to read long passages each day, but rather meditate on *what* you read. Let the truth of it soak into your mind, body and soul.

Prayer time might also involve reading *daily devotions*…devotional readings that will help you grow in your Christian faith.

Lastly, prayer time might include specific *personal prayers*…things that you, dear reader, want or need the shepherd's help with for that particular day.

Dear reader, we have "an open line" to heaven all the time, but we need to know who's on the other end of that open line! We need to know that Being personally…like we would a near and dear friend or loved one! We can only do that if we spend time with Him each day!

Prayer:

You have said, O Lord, that You are the good shepherd and that Your sheep know Your voice and follow You. We ask You, O Lord, to help us be one of Your sheep and to know Your voice. Help us to spend time with You each day, getting to know You better so that we can recognize and know Your voice, Your promptings, Your nudging, Your advice, Your directions. Increase in us a love for You, O Lord, so that Your voice will be familiar to us when it comes to us amidst our daily activities and involvements. Help us to have "open lines of communication" with You. We ask this in Your precious name because You are the good shepherd, You are the door of the sheep, You are...Jesus, and...You are my Lord and Savior.

Amen

A Sure Foundation

Dubbed "the dynamic duo" by a dear friend of ours, John and I shared the work of a lot of home projects. One year we decided to enlarge the garage…make our one-car garage into a two-car garage. Figuring that we could save some money if we dug the foundation ourselves, we started the digging. Our backyard sloped downward toward the back of the lot, so digging the foundation in the forefront of the foundation required more digging than in the back. Hours of digging brought us to the point that I was so far down in the hole that you couldn't see me, and John, from his vantage point inside the house, could only see a shovel full of dirt coming out of the hole!

Getting a little hot and tired, I thought about what it must have been like for grave diggers and how often they must have been exhausted by the time they'd dug deep enough for the coffin. I wondered what it felt like to lie down in such a space that far beneath the ground, so, putting the shovel aside, I laid down.

When John didn't see any more dirt flying out of the hole he came out to see what was going on and when he saw me lying in the hole he threw a couple of shovels full onto my legs! Well, with that the joke was over and I bounded out of there!

Finally, with the foundation completed, we hired builders for the rest of the task and it wasn't long before we had a new two-car garage.

The basis for our new two-car garage had to be a good foundation. And, as we look at the Christian religion we see that the cornerstone, *the sure foundation*, is Jesus Christ. In Isaiah 28: 16, of the Old Testament it says, *"Therefore thus says the Lord God, 'Behold, I am laying in Zion for a foundation a stone, a tested stone, a precious cornerstone, of a sure foundation.'"* Then, in the New Testament, references to those words are seen again (e.g., Romans 9:33, 1 Peter 2:4-6, Matthew 21:42, Mark 12:10, Luke 20:17, Acts 4:11 and Ephesians 2:20, to name a few).

Jesus is *the* foundation of the Christian religion and He should be *our* foundation, our *sure foundation*, as well!

In 1 Corinthians 3:11-15, it says, *"For no other foundation can any one lay than that which is laid, which is Jesus Christ. Now if any one builds on the foundation with gold, silver, precious stones, wood, hay, stubble-each man's work will become manifest; for the Day will disclose it, because it will be revealed with fire, and the fire will test what sort of work each one has done. If the work which any man has built on the foundation survives, he will receive a reward. If any man's work is burned up, he will suffer loss, though he himself will be saved, but only as through fire.* "

And, the verses which follow those words (1 Corinthians 3:18-19) say, *"Do you not know that you are God's temple and that God's spirit dwells in you? If any one destroys God's temple, God will destroy him. For God's temple is holy, and that temple you are."*

Thus, in those verses (1 Corinthians 3:11-19), we read that Christ should be the foundation of our lives. With Him as the foundation of our lives our bodies become God's temple and God's spirit dwells within us. God's temple is holy (and so are we! It's been said that, as believers in and followers of Christ, we are all saints, but just in different levels of perfection!)

If we try to build on the foundation of our lives with anything (i.e., as it says in those verses, gold, silver, precious stones, wood, hay or stubble) the results will be tested. Anything not grounded in and approved of by the Lord will not be able to stand the test.

Therefore, whatever "works" you do of a Christian nature, examine them carefully to determine *why* you are doing them. What are your motives? Are they grounded in the Lord? Would the Lord approve?

And, as regards your physical body, since it is God's temple and houses God's spirit, are there things that you're doing that are not grounded in the Lord or that the Lord would not approve of?

With Jesus Christ as the foundation of our lives our works and our physical bodies should reflect Him and His presence!

We all have areas of our lives that can be improved upon and changed. Not one of us is free from sin. It takes on a variety of appearances and degrees of involvement, anger, fault finding, greed, judging, lust, self-righteousness, conceit, extravagance, swearing, covetousness, bitterness, worry, and so on. None of us is sinless!

As it says in 1 John 1:8, *"If we say we have no sin, we deceive ourselves, and the truth is not in us."*

Nevertheless, we don't have to stay in a "woe is me, I'm a hopeless sinner" state of mind. We can confess our sins to the Lord, repent, and move onwards (and upwards!).

1 John 1:9, says, *"If we confess our sins, he is faithful and just, and will forgive our sins and cleanse us from all unrighteousness."*

Prayer:

In the name of the Father, Son, and Holy Spirit, amen. I come before You today, O God, to praise You for the fact that I am mysteriously and wonderfully made in Your image. I praise You that You created my body in Your image and that if I've asked Your son, Jesus Christ, to be the foundation of my life, *my sure foundation,* that He inhabits my body and that makes my body a holy temple where the spirit of God resides.

Help me to take care of my body, your temple, and to select wisely the works and involvements in my life…that I might add to the foundation in ways that are favored and approved of by You, O Lord.

Forgive me for the times when I sin and *do, say, or think* things that are not approved of by You. Help me to over-come the temptations of those things so that the next time they appear…I may be able to resist them.

All this I ask in Your precious Name.

Amen.

Devotional Reading #26

Fear

I love cats! However, my husband, John, won't let me have a cat. So…as a substitute, I have two ceramic cats! One ceramic cat is a Siamese cat and the other is…well…what…an alley cat? I've named those cats "Siam" and "Snicklefritz II." Siam and Snicklefritz II "spy out each other" from opposite ends of my display cabinet in the living room. The one ceramic cat, Siam, looks terribly apprehensive about the presence of the other cat, but the ceramic alley cat, Snicklefritz II, looks completely bored with it all as he stretches a *big* stretch. Well, I have to tell you, once in a while, I dust them!

My husband thinks those ceramic cats are the perfect cats for his house! They "stay put," don't require any food, don't scratch the furniture and don't make any messes. John's happy!

Over the years, people have given me those ceramic cats because they know I like cats. I even get cat greeting cards…sometimes I get them for Valentine's Day, sometimes I get them for my birthday, sometimes I get them because my friends just feel like buying me a "cat card." They're often funny cat cards and so I love to get them!

One summer a cat began sleeping on the roof of the neighbor's shed adjoining our backyard. I watched that cat over the course of the summer and began to think that maybe it was a feral cat (a cat gone "wild.") So, I started putting out a little food for it and then watched as it eagerly ate, but always with one eye on me. It was afraid of people!

As the weather got colder and colder I felt truly sorry for Mystic. I got John, my husband, to build a "cat house"...a wooden box about three feet by three feet with an opening and a piece of clear plexiglass on one side so it could go in and out and still see what was going on. I'd put the dish of food inside the cat house every day and gradually, it began to go inside "its house" to eat.

Summer turned into fall, fall into winter, and I was still feeding that cat. Gradually, as the weather turned colder and colder, I watched carefully to see where it came from...which direction. Where was it living? Then, one day I saw where it came from. Oh, my word! It was coming out of the sewer! It was a sewer cat, it was a homeless abandoned cat and it lived in the sewer! And so, dubbed "Mystic" for its name, it truly was a "mystery cat!"

Every day at roughly dusk, I'd watch Mystic come from the direction of the sewer two houses away, run down the sidewalk toward our house and go into that cat house to eat its food!

As the winter wore on and the snow piled up, I'd take the shovel and go to the corner sewer and dig away until the sewer opening was clear so Mystic could get out. (I'm sure the neighbors thought I was nuts! I suppose that's why they still, to this day, don't say much to me!)

Well, anyway, when the temperature went below zero, I got two heating pads, nailed one to the inside wall of that cat house and put the other one on the floor. With both pads plugged into our outside outlets, Mystic had a *heated* cat house!

I tried to get near enough to Mystic to touch it ("it" because I never was able to determine if it was male or female), but it never permitted me. I'd get within a foot of it, and then it would back up...always skeptical, always afraid.

Well, I loved that black and white Mystic cat! And, I think, if Mystic could have made it through that winter, maybe within another summer I could have tamed it, but I never got the chance. By February, there was so much snow that I'm sure living in the sewer that poor thing couldn't tell if it was day or night down there, it was so dark. Mystic's comings and goings became more and more erratic and Mystic looked sick. Finally, after coming one evening about nine o'clock when it was completely dark and the food had turned into hard pellets from the cold, it didn't come any more. I cried! My poor little sewer cat hadn't made it. My poor little Mystic had undoubtedly died!

In the Bible, in Luke 8:27-36, it tells about a disturbed, homeless man who lived, not in a house, but among the tombs. Such was not an unusual case, for in ancient times disturbed people sometimes took refuge among the tombs and that's why the cemeteries were often located far from town. The townspeople feared the spirits of the dead and the presence of such disturbed people as that homeless man.

The word "fear" has two meanings: 1) an apprehension of evil that normally leads someone to either flee or to fight, and 2) a sense of awe and reverence felt in the presence of a higher authority, be it parent, leader, or especially, God.

With the little sewer cat, Mystic, and with the townspeople who feared the disturbed homeless man, the first meaning of the word "fear" would apply. Mystic feared people and had no trust in someone who was trying to befriend him or help him. The townspeople feared the disturbed homeless man because he was violent and uncontrollable. In the case of the little sewer cat, its fear undoubtedly led to its demise. In the case of the disturbed homeless man, the townspeople were soon amazed to see him clothed and in his right mind because Jesus Christ freed him from a legion of demons that had possessed him.

As regards the second meaning of "fear," we are often told to "fear God" and it's this fear that is important for the remainder of this devotional reading.

In Psalm 111:9, we read (King James Version) *"He sent redemption unto his people: he hath commanded his covenant for ever: holy and reverend is his name."* But, then in the New International Version we read that same verse as: *"He provided redemption for his people; he ordained his covenant forever - holy and awesome is his name."* Other versions of the Bible use still different words, but the point that needs to be made is that gradually "fear of the Lord" came to mean "a good relationship with God, the second meaning of the word fear (stated in Psalm 111:9), rather than the first meaning.

A good relationship with God begins with a reverent sense that God is so powerful and righteous that we dare not take Him lightly. But, it goes on from there to mean "awe" and a sense of deep security. "Awe" meaning "respectful fear or wonderment that's deep, but which leads to security."

In Psalm 34:9, we read, *"O fear the Lord, you his saints, for those who fear him have no want!"*

Or in Psalm 111:10, we read, *"The fear of the Lord is the beginning of wisdom; a good understanding have all those who practice it, His praise endures for ever!"*

So, dear reader, if you've ever struggled with that phrase, "fear the Lord," you might substitute the words "have awe for the Lord," or a respectful fear, wonderment, or reverence for Him. And, because you have that "awe" for Him, He will keep you secure and in His care.

Prayer:
Oh, Lord, help me not to fear You, but to have an awesome respect and reverence for You. Help me to place my trust in You…that with trust comes wisdom and with wisdom comes security. You've said that You will never leave me nor forsake me. Help me to know that in the depths of my being!

Amen

Devotional Reading # 27

Faces

All of my life I'd had to answer the questions "What's the matter with your eye? What did you do to your eye?" To which I'd answer, "Nothing, I was born that way." And then I'd hear them say, "Oh, I'm sorry, I didn't know…"

Over the years I'd taught myself how to squint with the other eye so that, when photos were taken, my droopy eyelid wasn't quite so obvious.

I'd also been born without much of a chin and as I got older, especially from the side view, my face merged right into my neck region. Without the separation of a chin line, I looked years older than I was.

When I reached the age of fifty I decided to have a little cosmetic surgery to correct those problems; I decided to have a face lift. That surgery, however, turned out to be a pretty big deal, a lot bigger than I expected! I think it was a good thing that I hadn't known how extensive it was going to be and what was involved. If I had known, I don't think I would have gone through with the surgery. I wonder now how I ever had the nerve to do it! Ultimately, they snipped both eyelids and made my eyes look pretty much the same. No more would people ask me "What's the matter with your eye? What did you do to your eye?" Then, while they were at it, they snipped away the bags from under my eyes so I didn't look so tired all the time. They snipped around my ears and went into my cheek areas and tightened up my cheek muscles so my cheeks didn't sag. They lipo-suctioned my neck and gave me a chin, and they re-positioned my ears closer to my head.

And, when they were all finished with the surgery they bandaged up my head and said I could go home. Well, I have to tell you, dear reader, my husband took one look at me when I came from that surgery and he thought he'd married a "Ferengi" like those big headed creatures on Star Trek! He didn't say much as we headed home. Neither did I.

The next several days I spent in a darkened room with ice packs on my face to keep the swelling down. But, finally, enough time had passed and it was time to return to the doctor's office to get the bandages off. What a relief it was to get those bandages off and, when I got home, to wash the dried blood out of my hair! From then on it was an "upward trek" toward an "improved me," and within weeks I looked pretty good.

Today, many years after that facelift surgery, I'm still wondering how I had the nerve to do it, but I have to tell you, I'm mighty glad that I did! My appearance and my self image improved because of it. Nevertheless, would I do it again? Nope, not a chance! As a senior citizen, what you see is what you get!

In the world of portrait artists, the human face is of paramount importance, indeed, it may be the artist's livelihood. A good portrait artist is sought after by people who are willing to pay a premium price to have their likenesses recorded on canvas.

Before a portrait artist can achieve favorable notoriety, he must learn the mechanics of drawing the human head and face. He must learn the "planes of the head" and what's called "eye widths" to measure the proportions of the face. The planes of the head help the artist establish proportions and the placement of features. Eye widths make sure the size of the eyes is correct for the size of the face, as well as that the size of the forehead is correct for the size of the face, etc. The whole face can be divided into eye widths to get everything on the face to look proportionate and accurate. There are proper measuring and sighting techniques that the artist must know and use if the drawing is to look correct. Those techniques must be observed before individual characteristics can be drawn.

Individuals vary in the length, width and shape of their heads and faces…some are longer, some are shorter, some are square shaped, some heart shaped, etc., but the artist must know the basics before proceeding to draw a human head and face. Indeed, the human head and its face is a complex work of art, molded and crafted by an awesome creator!

In the Bible, there are many references to "faces." Indeed, the Bible mentions the "face of God," the "face of the Lord," a "king's face," the "face of an angel," the "face of man," etc.

However, in Exodus 29-35, we read an interesting account about Moses. *"When Moses came down from Mount Sinai, with the two tables of the testimony in his hand as he came down from the mountain, Moses did not know that the skin of his face shone because he had been talking with God. And when Aaron and all the people of Israel saw Moses, behold, the skin of his face shone, and they were afraid to come near him."*

Thus, when Moses had spoken with God, some of God's radiance had attached itself to Moses' face. Then, little by little, when he spoke with the people of Israel, God's radiance began to wane from Moses' face. And, because he did not want the people to see "God's radiance disappearing" or, as it says in 2 Corinthians 3: 13, "the end of the fading splendor," Moses put a veil over his face.

2 Corinthians 3: 14-18 goes on to say, *"But their minds were hardened; for to this day, when they read the old covenant, that same veil remains unlifted, **because only through Christ is it taken away.** (Emphasis added) Yes, to this day whenever Moses is read a veil lies over their minds; but when a man turns to the Lord the veil is removed. Now the Lord is the Spirit, and where the Spirit of the Lord is, there is freedom. And we all, with unveiled face, beholding the glory of the Lord, are being changed into his likeness from one degree of glory to another; for this comes from the Lord who is the Spirit."*

And in 2 Corinthians 4:3-4, we read, *"And even if our gospel is veiled, it is veiled only to those who are perishing. In their case the god of this world has blinded the minds of the unbelievers, to keep them from seeing the light of the gospel of the glory of Christ, who is the likeness of God."*

Jesus Christ unlocks the minds of people to important truths! Through Christ the veils of deception, untruths, fears and disbeliefs fall away. In John 14:6 Christ has said, *"I am the way, and the truth, and the life, no one comes to the Father, but by me."*

Christ is the answer!

You know, once in a while I think about that day when I'll stand before God in the heavenlies…when I'm standing before Him, face to face! How awesome that day will be! Even *more awesome* than what Moses experienced when He spoke with God, face to face, on Mount Sinai. I can't even begin to imagine how it will be to face God in His throne room in heaven!

And, how about you, dear reader? Have you ever thought about that day? Have you ever wondered how it will be? Will you, dear reader, be among the people who, *because you've invited Jesus Christ into your life as your Lord and Savior,* can look forward to that day when you'll face God in the heavenlies and behold His radiant face?

In Psalm 11:7, we read, *"the upright shall behold his face."*

If Jesus is the Lord of your life, dear reader, then you can rejoice in and find comfort in the words found in Numbers 6:24-26, *"The Lord bless you and keep you, the Lord make his face to shine upon you, and be gracious to you; the Lord lift up his countenance upon you, and give you peace."*

Prayer:
Oh, Lord Jesus, I know that I am a sinner and that I need Your forgiveness. I believe that You died on the cross for my sins so that they might be taken away from me. I want to turn away from those sins. I ask that You come into my heart and life today…to be "on the throne of my life." I want to trust you as my Savior and follow You as my Lord.

Help me, this day, O Lord, to remember the words of this reading and to live my life…this day…in such a way that some day I'll be able to stand in front of You in the heavenlies and look into Your awesome face!

Amen

Crowning Glory

In the Old Testament, Delilah was enticed by the Philistines to try and discover what was the source of Samson's strong power. In Judges 16:5-9, we read, *"... 'Entice him, and see wherein his great strength lies, and by what means we may overpower him, that we may bind him to subdue him; and we will each give you eleven hundred pieces of silver.' And Delilah said to Samson, 'Please tell me wherein your great strength lies, and how you might be bound, that one could subdue you.'*

And Samson said to her, 'If they bind me with seven fresh bowstrings which have not been dried, then I shall become weak, and be like any other man.' Then the lords of the Philistines brought her seven fresh bowstrings which had not been dried, and she bound him with them. Now she had men lying in wait in an inner chamber. And she said to him, 'The Philistines are upon you, Samson!' But he snapped the bowstrings, as a string of two snaps when it touches the fire. So the secret of his strength was not known."

Reading onwards in Judges, finally, in chapter 16:17, we read, *"... 'A razor has never come upon my head; for I have been a Nazarite to God from my mother's womb. If*

I be shaved, then my strength will leave me, and I shall become weak, and be like any other man.' When Delilah saw that he had told her all his mind, she sent and called the lords of the Philistines, saying, 'Come up this once, for he has told me all his mind.' Then the lords of the Philistines came up to her, and brought the money in their hands. She made him sleep upon her knees; and she called a man, and had him shave off the seven locks of his head. Then she began to torment him, and his strength left him."

Dear reader, you can read the conclusion to that story by referring to Judges 16:20-31.

In that story of Samson we've seen the importance of his hair. It was *so* important to him!

Not that I'm to be identified with or likened to that great man, Samson, in any way whatsoever, but for a woman, the hair on her head is extremely important too. A woman's hair has often been referred to as "her crowning glory."

Born with naturally curly brown hair, as I got older and my hair got whiter and whiter, I didn't like the fact that I looked older than my actual years. In fact, I was one of those women who would probably have dyed her hair brown until the day she died if it hadn't been for one thing…I developed an allergy to hair coloring! I switched to using a hair "rinse" instead of a "dye" and that worked fine except for one thing…my hair always seemed to end up *red*! On me, I don't like red hair! On other people…yes, but me…no! And, so one day I decided that I'd had enough, I was going to strip all of the color out of my hair and "start over" if you will. I bought a bottle of "stripper," read the directions, and dumped it on my head. Now, something definitely went wrong, because when I rinsed that stuff off, I was shocked at the color of my hair!

Dear reader, I have to tell you, at the age of 61, with that hair color, if I'd added a ring through my nose and maybe an eyebrow ring, I could have dated a Harley Davidson biker and fit right in! My hair was "punker yellow!" I don't mean blonde, I mean "punker yellow"…*yellow*…like *bright* yellow!

Well, obviously I had a problem! John was watching TV in the living room and I didn't dare to let him see me! I sneaked into the bedroom, dug out my wig from the bottom drawer, plopped it on my head and, hiding behind the dining room wall, announced to John that I'd made a "slight error in judgment" and needed to go to the drug store!

At the drug store, I stood there reading all of the boxes of hair coloring products. None of them sounded like they could help me with my problem! In the event that I'd missed one, I reread the boxes and was there so long that the clerk came over and asked, "Is there something that I can help you with?"

Sheepishly, I lifted up a corner of my wig and pulled down a strand of punker yellow hair. "Yes, perhaps you can help me. I've made a terrible mistake in coloring my hair and now I have this awful punker-style yellow hair! How can I get rid of this and get it back to being brown?"

"Oh," she said, "almost any one of those products will cover that up."

"Yes," I said, "I know that, but I can't use them because I'm allergic to the peroxide in hair dye."

"Well," she said, "I don't know how else you're going to cover it up."

Thus, fed up with rinses and having no other alternative, I bought a dye...a brown hair dye, drove home, read and reread the directions, and ultimately dumped it all on my head.

With the addition of that brown dye...I'd actually dumped a *double dose of peroxide* on my head within a couple of hours! And, as I suspected, in the ensuing hours, which turned into weeks, I suffered! Oooooh, my goodness, did I suffer! *Big time!* My head broke out in hives...little bumps...that itched something terrible! My ears swelled up until they stuck out like two cauliflowers were stuck to the sides of my head! I, indeed, had "cauliflower ears!"

And...itch! Oh, it was awful! The only time I had any relief from the itching was when I was in the shower with the water running on my head and it got so that whenever John couldn't find me...I was in the shower, again! I took two and three showers a day! Ahhh...sweet relief!

Well, I have to tell you, that was it! That ended it for me! I knew I was beaten! I gave up! No more hair coloring for me, no sir! I was done! Finished! That's it! I'd had it!

And so, over the course of some six months, as my *real* hair color began to grow out, I didn't look so good! I stayed home a lot!

And so...little by little I joined the ranks of the "white haired little old ladies!" And, I have to tell you, dear reader, it's been a *big* adjustment for me! In fact, once before I'd tried to "go natural" and I hadn't made it! I couldn't take it! I'd look in the mirror and say "Who dat?" And, so, I'd colored my hair again.

People treat you differently when you look older, do you know that? Yup, it happens…especially when you've got white hair! Some of the treatments are good (senior discounts at the movies and restaurants…but, now I don't have to show them my driver's license to prove my age… they *know* I'm old enough!) and some of the treatments aren't so good. But, yup! No doubt about it…"getting older" takes some getting used to!

Another thing I began to notice was that the other little old ladies looked differently at me. I noticed that they kind of cocked their heads to one side, looked at me with a quizzical look, and I thought I could hear them thinking "Hmmmmm, I wonder if I know her. She looks kind of familiar…"

In the New Testament, in Matthew 10: 29-31, it tells us that when a sparrow dies, its death is known to the Father in heaven and that we are of far more value and worth to Him than many sparrows, *to the point that even the hairs on our head are numbered by Him!* God knows the very hairs of our heads…He even has them numbered!

Thus, this side of glory we sometimes talk of the hair on our heads as being "our crowning glory" but throughout the Bible there are various kinds of "crowns" spoken about, i.e., a crown of righteousness (2 Timothy 4:8), a crown of life (James 1:12, and Revelation 2:10), a golden crown (Revelation 4:4 and 9:7), a crown of twelve stars (Revelation 12:13), a perishable wreath of crown (1 Colossians 9:25), a crown of thorns (Matthew 27:29, Mark 15:17, and John 19:2), and in 1 Peter 5:4, *a crown of glory* is mentioned, although it refers to something other than a person's hair. Indeed, in the Bible there are references made to crowns set with gems, royal crowns (worn by kings and queens), priestly crowns (worn by the priests) and victor's crowns.

Ultimately, dear reader, all of the crowns, whatever they are, whatever we've managed to inherit or acquire here on earth, they must all give way to the *crown of eternal life* which, if Jesus is our Lord and Savior, we will be given when we go before God in heaven. In Revelation 2:10, it says, *"...Be faithful unto death, and I will give you the crown of life"* (Those words were spoken to the church in Smyrna, the suffering church, in what is, today, modern Turkey). In James 1:12, it says, *"Blessed is the man who endures trial, for when he has stood the test he will receive the crown of life which God has promised to those who love him."* Those "crowns of life" may not be something put upon our heads but rather our whole bodies, as we will be *"crowned with life...eternal life!"* That "crown" will be *the real crowning glory!* To that end we must all strive, hope for and look forward to! What an awesome day that will be!

Prayer:
Oh heavenly Father, help me this day to live my life in such a way that, when day has ended, I can lie down to sleep and know that Your favor rests on me! Help me this day to remember that whatever "crowns" I receive or achieve this day, that they pale by comparison to the crown of eternal life I will receive someday when I stand, with the other saints down through the ages, before You seated on Your throne in the heavenlies.

Amen

Worth a Thousand Words

It's often said that "a picture is worth a thousand words."

Dear reader, is there a particular picture that you've come across in your life that you feel is worth a thousand words? Perhaps you've found one that you liked so much that you purchased it and have it hanging on a wall in your home?

Of course, there are many types of pictures and paintings, plus many artistic styles, so a choice must be made based on what appeals to you. Do you like bold colors? Or perhaps more gentle, pastel colors appeal to you? Do you like abstract art? Or perhaps you prefer still life or maybe scenes of nature? What?

As a child, I was given two pictures that I loved looking at and which always brought a smile to my face. They were both pictures that made me feel good when I looked at them. The first one was a drawing of a "Schmoo," a funny looking armless pear-shaped character that was introduced into Al Capp's "Li'l Abner" comic strip back in 1948. That funny looking character became an American sensation and readership of the comic strip more than doubled as America became "Schmoo-struck."

The Schmoo was a being that loved humans, laid eggs and bottles of Grade A milk…a being that loved humans so much that it would become a sizzling steak if its owner even looked a little hungry! During the first year of its appearance in the comic strip Schmoo merchandise generated over $25,000,000. Then, its presence spilled over into the Presidential race of 1948 followed by the U.S. Government producing a Schmoo savings bond in 1949. Candy-chocked Schmoos were air dropped into West Berlin in 1948 by the 17th Military Airport Squadron. Even today, as I write this, there are about 62,000 entries for "Schmoos" on the Internet!

But for me, as a child, I knew none of the above. I just liked looking at that picture of a Schmoo! It made me feel good! I could laugh right out loud just looking at that silly Schmoo!

The other picture I loved as a child was known as "The Gay Philosopher." The artist of that painting was Henry Major, a well known caricature artist in the 1940's whose "Philosopher" painting bore a striking resemblance to the artist, himself. It showed a funny looking man with a crinkled old black hat on his head, a white shirt with a stand up collar, a shoestring thin tied tie, and a brownish-red jacket. But, what had caught my attention as a child and the reason that I loved that painting so much was…the face! The "Gay Philosopher" had a twinkle in his eyes, puffy cheeks, and a grin on his face that said he might have just been caught with his hand in the cookie jar, but most important...he didn't care! His face showed such contentment and lack of worry!

I'd look at that painting and it just made me feel good! I felt happiness and contentment just looking at it!

I guess other people must have felt the same way when they looked at that painting because the Brown and Bigelow Company in the Twin Cities of Minnesota picked up the "Gay Philosopher series" and put out a calendar featuring them. That series became number two in popularity, right behind the series done by Norman Rockwell (Rockwell's Boy Scouts and the Four Seasons calendars).

Nevertheless, by the time that I'd become an adult, married John, my husband, and moved into our home, I had another painting that I loved. I loved to look at it because the message and significance was so profound and important. Consequently, we decided that that painting should be the first item we carried into our new home and displayed on the wall. It was a painting of the United Nations Building in New York City with the flags of the various countries out in front. But the most important part of the painting was the "building size figure" of Jesus Christ knocking on the side of the building!

The painting, titled, "Prince of Peace" was painted by the artist, Harry Anderson, who was one of the nation's top religious illustrators in the 40's and 50's, providing illustrations for such magazines as *Collier's, The Saturday Evening Post,* and *Woman's Home Companion.* Mr. Anderson excelled in paintings that placed Jesus in settings such as hospitals and offices.

If we look in the Bible for the term "Prince of Peace" it can be found in the Old Testament, in Isaiah 9:6. There we read the words, *"For to us a child is born, to us a son is given; and the government will be upon his shoulder, and his name will be called Wonderful, Counselor, Mighty God, Everlasting Father, Prince of Peace."*

Revelation 3:20, says, *"Behold, I stand at the door and knock; if any one hears my voice and opens the door, I will come in to him and eat with him, and he with me."* Jesus continues to knock at the doors of earth's nations just as He does at the hearts of the people.

Another picture I have in my home I cut out of a magazine. Its message also spoke to me! Circular in scope, in the picture's center is Jesus Christ on the cross, but the view is looking down from above. Christ's head is bowed downwards and there's a concerned Roman soldier looking up at Jesus. The caption for the picture is: "Behold, The Lamb of God." And in the Bible we find references to that in John 1:29, where it says, *"Behold, the Lamb of God, who takes away the sin of the world!"* Jesus became the paschal lamb who was sacrificed! (1 Corinthians 5:7).

Finally, I want to comment on one more picture I have in my home that I think "is worth a thousand words." I'm afraid that I don't know who the artist was nor the painting's title, but the message is a profound one! In the foreground are the throngs of humanity. They are on one side of a deep, fiery chasm and on the other side of the chasm is an oasis with green grass, trees and a lake. Then, coming from amidst the throngs of humanity is a huge wooden cross that leads upwards. Above the top of the cross is Jesus Christ with His arms outstretched, beckoning to humanity to come to Him via that cross! The cross provides the way to avoid falling into that deep, fiery chasm!

Dear reader, in this devotional reading I've described five pictures, paintings, if you will, that I've felt were "worth a thousand words." The first two, when I was a child, brought me joy and laughter. They were fun to look at! The other three were religious in nature and their messages were profound. Taken together, those five pictures might represent something of "life!"

A childlike cartoon caricature like a "Schmoo" represented fantasy and carefree fun. The "Gay Professor" was a whimsical character who exemplified the idea that "None of us is perfect, but the worst of it is, some of us are impossible." The Professor wasn't concerned about worrying, but rather, looked on the bright side of life, and either enjoyed it or accepted it!

The "Prince of Peace" continues to knock at the door of our hearts and even if we've invited Him into our lives as our Lord and Savior, He continues to seek us. The choice is ours, we can either go deeper with Him, spend more time with Him, love Him more, serve Him better, or we can turn away from Him. He wants us to have an abundant and good life.

He is "The Lamb of God" and He laid down His life so that we might have that abundant and good life. He forgives us when our choices aren't good ones and we confess them to Him. He cleanses us from all unrighteousness and sets us free.

But, like the throngs of humanity that we're a part of...there's only one way to receive eternal life after death and that's by way of the cross. We must come to Him over that cross.

Life is somewhat like a composite of those five pictures (and I'm sure other wonderful pictures and paintings could be added to make the composite more complete, but for simplicity's sake, I've kept the reading centered on those five pictures.).

And now, what about you, dear reader? What's been going through your mind as you've read this devotional reading? Have you "gotten my drift?"

Prayer:
Heavenly, Father, I come before You today to thank You for the life You've given me. I thank You for the joyful and fun times, the whimsical times, the more serious times. Lord, I thank You for all of it. I thank You for the knowledge that because of You I can look forward to eternal life…that I don't have to be fearful of whatever comes my way because ultimately, if You're my Lord and Savior, I will go on from this world to a far better place. Help me to cling to that cross, because it's the way to You.

Amen

Life

The human body is remarkable! The heart beats 103,689 times during an average day. The heart pumps the blood some 168,000,000 miles in the same length of time. The body generates some 450 foot-tons of power and a person breathes 23,040 times. The body uses over 7,000,000 brain cells and speaks some 4,800 words in addition to moving more than 750 major body muscles.

I am oversimplifying life by far, but to kids, life each day seems filled with endless hours of schooling, plus listening, learning, doing, and playing in a variety of activities. To adults, life is filled with working, making decisions, families, errands, and responsibilities. To older adults, life is filled with hobbies, traveling, enjoyments, being alone, and health issues.

In twenty-first century living, there seems little time for relaxation and taking it easy. There are many demands placed on people. The advent of computers, cell phones, fast-paced movies, TV, and games, plus other choices people are required to make, all add up to a fast-paced lifestyle. Today, we often hear about road rage, abuses, corporate greed and corruptions, job layoffs, and unemployment. Companies continually downsize, if not totally dissolve. On the nightly news we often hear about violent crimes, wars, and terrorism. We hear about disasters and calamities. We hear about deviant lifestyles. We hear about the rising and falling of the stock market. And on and on it goes.

Worldwide, there seems to be very little peace or contentment in the hearts of people. People have everything, and yet, they seem to have nothing. They are empty…often unhappy, discontented, perplexed, stressed out, and angry. And, why is that? In twenty-first century America, when life should be so good for people, why are so many people that way?

And, how about you, dear reader? Are you happy in life? Do you know your purpose for living?

As the author of this book, I have to tell you that I was 31 years old before I became a born-again Christian. At that age I asked Jesus Christ into my life as my personal Lord and Savior and I became a changed person. I became happier, more peaceful, more content. My purpose in life took on new meaning for me and, while I'm still a "work in progress," the Lord Jesus has been working with me and through me ever since. May He continue to do so. Dear reader…I'd like to invite you to seek Him further in your life. Go deeper with Him. Pray to Him on a daily basis. Find times to be with Him in the course of the day. Read His Word, the Bible. Meditate on His word. Talk to Him about things that trouble or perplex you. Listen for His promptings and "nudgings" ...He'll guide you and direct you. Trust Him.

In conclusion, I think this poem pretty well sums up life (taken from my dad's book, *Youthful Ideas for Devotions*).

> Life is not what has been,
> But what it might become.
> Life is not what we have done,
> But what we are going to do.
> Life is not what was done Yesterday,
> But what is going to be done Today,
> Tomorrow, and the next day.
> Life is compassion, life is serving,
> Life is giving and life is living
> To the fullest each day!

May the words of that poem live in your heart!

Devotional Reading #31

Thoughts to Ponder

A smile costs nothing, but creates much. It happens in a flash, but the memory lasts forever. It cannot be bought, begged, borrowed, or stolen, and it is of no earthly good to anyone until it is given away. So if you are in a hurry and you meet someone who is too weary to give it back to you, leave one of your best with that person, for no one needs a smile quite as much as he who has none to give.

+

It's nice to be important,
but it's more important to be nice.

+

It's better to remain silent and be thought
a fool than to speak and remove all doubt.

+

People are like steamboats:
they toot loudest when in a fog.

+
+

Knowing the right answers isn't enough,
you have to be able to use them.
Recipes don't bake cakes.

+

It isn't how much you know,
but how you use what you do know.

+

The sure way of getting the last word
in an argument is to say, "You're right!"

+

And, lastly, if you enjoyed reading this book by Susan Daniels Poulos, you might like to read another booklet by her, titled, *"Once Upon a Prayer...or Living 'Tween Two Denominations."* It's a happy book.

E-mail Susan for a copy: Yannisuep@aol.com.

Printed in the United States
36976LVS00003B/1-129